LEE HANEY'S ULTIMATE
BODYBUILDING

LEE HANEY'S
ULTIMATE
BODYBUILDING

LEE HANEY
WITH JIM ROSENTHAL

PHOTOGRAPHS BY J. M. MANION

St. Martin's Press

NEW YORK

Permission to use drawings on p. 24, taken from the *Manual of Structural Kinesiology, 10th Edition* by Clem W. Thompson, published by Mosby-Year Book Co., is granted by J.B. Lippincott Company.

Editor: George Witte
Copyedited by Eric C. Meyer
Design by Susan Hood

ISBN 0-312-09322-5

First Edition: June 1993
10   9   8   7   6   5   4

Books are available in quantity for promotional or premium use. Write to Director of Special Sales, St. Martin's Press, 175 Fifth Avenue, New York, NY 10010, for information on discounts and terms, or call toll-free (800) 221-7945. In New York, call (212) 674-5151 (ext. 645).

CONTENTS

ACKNOWLEDGMENTS

This book is dedicated to my father, Dorthel Lee Haney, who passed away on August 10, 1992. He gave me the support and caring I needed to fulfill all my goals in life. In my early days as an aspiring bodybuilder, he spent endless hours driving me from one competition to another, never complaining, always caring for me as a friend and as a son. His dedication and love served as the underlying force behind my success.

—Lee Haney

For Diane and Cyrene; their friendship is truly an inspiration. Thanks to Trisha Malin for her hard work. Martin Withrow, creative art director at FLEX, deserves credit for assisting me in selecting and cropping the photographs. And special thanks to George Witte, an editor who is always supportive and constructive.

—Jim Rosenthal

1

MY PERSONAL EVOLUTION IN BODYBUILDING

Being Number One has always been my goal in life. Breaking Arnold Schwarzenegger's record wasn't something that just happened by accident; it was the product of twenty years of hard work in the gym. And it all began with a simple journey—a trial-and-error adventure in lifting weights, doing cardiovascular exercise, and dieting for competitive success.

As an eight-time Mr. Olympia, many people look up to me as the man who knows everything about weight training. But no one has all the answers! Let's just say that I have an understanding of what it takes to be successful in the gym: Commitment, Dedication, Sensitivity, The hunger to be the very best!

Even the most accomplished lifter, though, begins his personal journey with nothing but the desire for success; a vision that motivates and sustains the training experience through all the ups and downs. The key is to trust your imagination; visualize your ideal physique. Focus on transforming your body according to your ambition—that commitment to work wonders with your God-given talent.

Now I must admit that God blessed me with superior genetics—a slim waist, big arms, a big back and chest, perfect symmetry and proportion. But getting a leg up genetically does not ensure competitive achievement in bodybuilding. In the final analysis, it's up to you to decide how hard you're willing to work to fulfill your dream.

My dream took shape on a South Carolina Christmas morning in 1971. I was only twelve at the time—Christmas was a very special occasion in the Haney household. I opened my presents and to my delight discovered a set of plastic dumbbells and barbells. That did it for me right then and there: I was hooked for life. I lifted with those plastic weights at least four days a week. I immediately noticed changes in my body, but I was just a young kid—what did I really know about bodybuilding?

My big goal as a teenager was to be as macho as possible. I looked up to Arnold and Robby Robinson, the premier bodybuilders of the *Pumping Iron* era of the 1970s. And I spent many Saturday afternoons looking in wonder at Steve Reeves in those amazing *Hercules* movies; his enormous physique and personal power really impressed me. I wanted to strut my stuff and carve out my own niche, but I didn't have a clue how to do it.

Playing football was my first brush with competitive success. The high school coach took me aside one day and asked if I'd try out for the team—I guess all my weight training was beginning to make an impression. Of course, by now I was lifting real weights in an actual weight room. I waxed a lot of the other top players, what with my muscle strength and size. I also played basketball, ran the 100-meter dash and threw the shot put and discus. I loved competing in sports and always worked hard to perform at my personal best.

And all of this athletic activity was paying off in solid muscle mass. I was getting bigger and looking better. Bodybuilding was a natural outlet for my consistency in the weight room.

At a local Nautilus center in Spartanburg, I entered a competition and won—no problem. Then I tried my hand at the Mr. South Carolina show and got waxed in a big way—I don't think I even placed in the top five or six.

Despite having my clock cleaned by a bunch of older guys, everyone encouraged me to pursue bodybuilding. I was only sixteen years old, and yet, I still managed to hold my own against the cream of the South Carolina crop. After that period of time, I must admit that I became really intrigued by the sport of bodybuilding—not possessed, mind you, but intrigued. I liked what it did to my physique. I liked the way it made me feel. And I enjoyed the competition.

Frankly, I prefer individual sports, activities where you compete against yourself. Now there's a lot you can learn from team sports—camaraderie, sportsmanship, sacrifice. But I hate pulling other people's slack. In body-building, though, it's Lee Haney against Lee Haney. Total discipline for the sake of success—that's the way I like it.

My life revolved around my training program. No more evenings killing time at the movies. No partying with friends. What a fantastic outlet for my adolescent fury and raw energy! Lifting weights kept me out of trouble. It taught me physical awareness. It forced me to take good care of myself and respect the sanctity of my body. No drugs for Lee Haney; I'd never do anything to hinder my development as an athlete or as a person.

Don't get the impression that I did nothing but lift weights twenty-four hours a day. I was always conscious of the importance of getting a good education. But suppose bodybuilding was the answer? What if I was able to turn it into a career? If that happened, I still wanted to give my life a sense of value beyond just pushing and pulling weights.

And so I studied and read everything I could get my hands on, always trying to better myself in school. I was not an A student, but I gave it my best shot. I'd alternate working out with doing my homework. It was a labor of love, really; I was happy just for the opportunity to realize my potential, and to put myself in a position to help people in a substantive way.

Lee Haney at age 17.

That's one of the reasons I turned to bodybuilding. I had a special gift. Why should I pass up the chance to make a name for myself? Not surprisingly, children look up to someone with an imposing physical presence—when Lee Haney talks, young people listen. I discovered this early on as a youth counselor in Spartanburg. I knew that if I made it big in bodybuilding, I'd have a shot at reaching young people with a positive message: to stay out of trouble and follow the right path.

Children need to get encouragement from the people they care about the most. That's very important. My family always told me I was special. The idea that you're special sort of grows on you, gives you a sense of self-esteem and meaning. Hey, you can do whatever you want in life, but you have to be willing to work for it.

Believe me, I'm no slouch when it comes to sweating and striving. I picked up extra money in high school by laying bricks, cutting lawns and washing dishes. There's nothing wrong with a good day's honest labor.

Honest labor is one thing, self-defeating toil is another. A man has to make many important decisions in his life, and one of the big ones for me was determining whether to seek full-time employment or go to Livingstone College in Salisbury, North Carolina, on a football scholarship. My coach told me I had until September to sort things out. So during that summer I went around to check out the local factories, the kind of places I'd be working at if I didn't go to college. The scene I saw inside the factory scared me half to death. Here were many of the guys I'd looked up to when I was a kid; these men were working really hard—sweat was pouring off them, smoke was flying all over the place. Man, it looked like a bleak forecast for the next twenty or thirty years.

This scary scene really blew my mind. I checked out another factory and saw the same awful images. That did it! I decided to grab that scholarship while the going was good. "Coach, please give it to me; I want that scholarship in the worst possible way." I knew that a college education would mean a lot, whether I made it as a professional bodybuilder or not.

So off I went to Livingstone, poised to blend physique building, football playing, and studying into my lifestyle. It didn't take long, though, before my plans went awry. A nagging ankle injury (a keepsake from my final football season at Broom High School) made playing college football painful and, finally, impossible. My mind snapped back to the factory—smoke, steam, forty years of pain—and was I worried. I called my high school guidance counselor, James "Pee Wee" Lambert, to see if he had any solutions.

"Pee Wee" Lambert saved my life. He made some calls and within twenty-four hours had secured a place for me—tuition and fees taken care of by the state of South Carolina—at Spartanburg Methodist College. Perfection! I could focus on my training, work a part-time job, and pursue my interest in youth counseling.

This was the crucial transition year in my life. Football was out of the picture. But the athletic side of me was still hungry; I needed another avenue for that energy. I remembered how well I'd done in that bodybuilding show at sixteen. Could I make a living as a professional bodybuilder? That question dogged me for weeks.

I distinctly remember discussing this subject with my father. I told him I was tired of being banged around the football field and wanted to try my hand at bodybuilding. He asked me, "Son, are there any financial rewards in bodybuilding?" And I really couldn't answer that question. I didn't know anything about bodybuilding as a business. But my mom and dad supported my decision to enter the bodybuilding world—as long as I continued to attend college. The die was cast; now it was up to me to rock and roll my way to the top.

I decided to test the waters at the Mr. Palmetto Contest in Greenville, South Carolina. It was just a local event, but I won it hands down. Then, at the tender age of eighteen, I pulled off a stunning upset at the Mr. South show in Charleston. This was not in the Teenage Division, mind you, but in the main bracket. I was just a young turk, but I defeated quite a few of the best bodybuilders in the South.

At nineteen, with an extra year of experience under my belt, I entered the Mr. Teenage America contest in Detroit. This was a very emotional time in my life. Shirley, my future wife and best friend in the world, offered invaluable assistance and support. All the guys at the Nautilus Fitness Center in Spartanburg, especially John Lankford, the owner, helped me put on a seminar to raise money for expenses—

Lee and Shirley.

they believed I was the only one at the gym who could make it out of there and go on to greatness.

Seventy-eight teenagers from around the United States pulled into Motown with a dream. After the smoke had cleared, I'd won both the heavyweight division and the overall show prize. That night I became the best teenage bodybuilder in America. A 212-pound wonder. Man, I was on top of the world. Bodybuilding greats like Frank Zane, Lou Ferrigno and Chris Dickerson had started their careers with wins at the Mr. Teenage America. Now it was my turn to take a shot at the brass ring.

Next stop was the Mr. USA contest in 1980. I went into that show at 218 pounds—I was steadily gaining weight through diet and training—and placed fourth. Not a bad performance. I wasn't disappointed; instead, I redoubled my efforts to break new ground in the sport. In the early stages of a career it's essential to fight back from defeat with fresh resolve.

Little did I know that I was headed for a temporary setback. Though I completed my degree in youth counseling at Spartanburg Methodist, 1981 was a very tough year for Lee Haney. I developed a cyst on my left wrist. Each time I'd try to bench press, the pain was unbearable. I handled this injury the right way, however, I had no intention of freaking out and doing something stupid. I had the cyst removed and rested until I was cleared by my doctors to lift again. Everything was cool. I was at peace with myself. But I would not let this downtime mess with my master plan.

I sat down with Shirley and Mark Bates, who was one of my training partners, and made a very definite commitment to fulfill a promise, a mark of honor: I told them that in 1982 I would shock the world of bodybuilding. No doubt about it; the bodybuilding world would stand up and take note of Lee Haney in 1982.

So what happened? A quick review of '82: I entered the Atlantic USA in Atlanta, Georgia, and won easily. That victory paved the way for the Junior Nationals in New Orleans—no sweat, I won that show with ease. A few months later I nailed the NPC (National Physique Committee) Nationals in New York on my first try, which enabled me to enter the Mr. Universe in Brussels, Belgium. So I was off to Belgium to snag the Mr. Universe title—and . . . I won that show too!

I was undefeated in '82. That was a great feeling of satisfaction and vindication. I had indeed shocked the world of bodybuilding, just as I planned and predicted. I'd put my heart and soul into my training, and was very happy and gratified that everything fell into place.

You can learn as much from failure as you can from success. Sure, I enjoyed dominating the competition in '82, but I really hit a crossroads in 1983 after placing third in my first Mr. Olympia, the World Series of bodybuilding events.

Yes, I was disappointed. I went into the show at 233 pounds, in great shape, I thought; but I came up short on the presentation side of the package. I was the biggest man on stage; in my mind that meant I was the best man on stage. In truth, though, I needed to refine my posing routine.

I remember running into Arnold at the '83 Olympia in Munich, Germany. I told him how frustrated I was with the outcome. He took me by the arm and asked me to focus my energy on learning from my mistakes. He expressed his opinion in classic "Arnold" fashion. "Lee, Lee, Lee—calm down and don't worry, you've got what it takes. You will be Mr. Olympia!" Little did either of us know at the time that I would one day break his record for consecutive and total Mr. Olympia titles.

2

ON THE ROAD TO MAKING HISTORY: THE MR. OLYMPIA ERA IN REVIEW

After the 1983 Olympia I decided to take Arnold's advice and direct my mind and body toward victory. After all, Jim Manion and Winston Roberts, two of the top judges in the IFBB (International Federation of Bodybuilding), had told me that I could win—that I would win—if I worked on my posing and trained with 100 percent intensity and focus.

In retrospect, 1983 was not such a bad year. Shirley and I had finally gotten married—we'd been sweethearts since the second grade—and that was a wonderful feeling. A week after the wedding I won my first professional show, the Night of Champions in New York City. Then I pulled off a major victory at the Caesar's Palace Grand Prix in Atlantic City during the filming of *Pumping Iron II—The Women.* Not too shabby. I'd won a couple of professional shows, waxed my share of athletes, and moved on with my training. Now was the time to really get serious.

When I say serious, I'm talking about working out with Rick Gianone, one of my all-time favorite training partners. Rick is totally crazy—crazy in the sense that he has boundless enthusiasm for lifting very heavy weights and eating a lot of good food. I have to be careful not to go overboard when I'm hanging out with Rick—he's extreme in the amount of food he can put away and the amount of weight he can hoist.

But gaining weight—and keeping it on—was one of my goals for the 1984 Olympia. I recall Arnold telling me two weeks before the '83 Olympia, "Lee, you look incredible at two hundred and forty pounds!" Unfortunately, I lost about ten pounds in the final ten days leading up to the show. I didn't know how to maintain my size, what with the time change, dealing with a long flight to Germany, and my lack of experience. No one can predict how your body will react to travel. There are so many variables to consider. I count myself lucky that I was as much as 233 pounds on that night in Munich.

Okay, so now I had something to prove—that I could maintain my size and peak for the big event. One of the things to understand about bodybuilding is that it's a personal challenge. You train consistently for so long and then everything boils down to one event, one night of drama that will make you or break you.

I want to share my personal reminiscence of each of my eight Mr. Olympia victories. I'm not doing this to brag or to revel in past glory—that's not my style. Everything in bodybuilding is a learning experience. I want you to know where I've been, and how I arrived at the top of the sport, to better understand the price of success. After the trip through Mr. Olympia history is complete, you'll be ready to train with me in the gym, to share the ultimate workout programs culled from eight years of trial and error, sweat and pain, exhilaration and satisfaction.

THE 1984 MR. OLYMPIA: RADIO CITY MUSIC HALL, NEW YORK CITY

It was over as soon as I hit the stage. I was harder and bigger than ever before, and still cut like a knife. I came in at 243 pounds—perfect. Despite my total confidence in my physique and posing, it was still a very competitive situation—the prejudging comparisons seemed to last forever. I was up against Samir Bannout, the 1983 Mr. Olympia, whose legs and arms seemed smaller than the year before; Mohamed Makkawy, who waxed me at the '83 Olympia with his posing brilliance; Jusup Wilkosz, the massive German Goliath; Albert Beckles, always ripped, always ready; and Sergio Oliva, a bodybuilding legend on the comeback trail. Though Sergio lacked my crispness and hardness, his body looked impressive—and he was well past fifty at the time!

Lee, Boyer Coe (left), and Mohamed Makkawy (right), pose off.

The competition was fierce, but I arrived on stage like a humungozoid and that was the beginning of my reign as bodybuilding's King of the Hill. Heck, I was just a baby at twenty-four. It felt like I could go on as Mr. Olympia forever.

Final Results:

1) Lee Haney
2) Mohamed Makkawy
3) Jusup Wilkosz
4) Albert Beckles
5) Roy Callender
6) Samir Bannout
7) Bob Paris
8) Sergio Oliva
9) Tom Platz
10) Bob Birdsong

THE 1985 MR. OLYMPIA: BRUSSELS, BELGIUM

At 242 pounds I could not be beat. I'd worked very hard on my posing after winning the '84 show. Doing exhibitions and being on stage with regularity improved my presentation and confidence. The audience feedback at those shows taught me an important lesson: I knew when to drop something from my routine that just didn't work. I'd also learned from my mistakes in the '83 Olympia. Back then, I didn't understand how to make adjustments in my diet to compensate for the time change. At five-feet-eleven-inches and 242 pounds, my calves, arms, and shoulders were thicker than in '84. I trained at a friend's gym in Germany the week before the Olympia, and that prepared me for the ultimate test of my ability—could I repeat as champion?

Rich Gaspari, Beckles, and Mike Christian were all gunning for my title. But I had worked too hard all year to make any mistakes. In the final analysis, though, the only person who could have beaten Lee Haney was Lee Haney.

Final Results:

1) Lee Haney
2) Albert Beckles
3) Richard Gaspari
4) Mohamed Makkawy
5) Mike Christian
6) Berry DeMey
7) Tom Platz
8) Sergio Oliva
9) Bob Paris
10) Frank Richard

THE 1986 MR. OLYMPIA: COLUMBUS, OHIO

Some people have said I was in the best shape of my life at this Olympia—well, that's not quite true. I peaked one week before the show, not on the night of the event. A little background: Jim Manion, one of the IFBB judges, was in Atlanta shortly before the contest. I asked him to critique my physique and he told me that I was in excellent shape, even better than in '84 and '85. But when I hit the stage he did not see the same guy. Yes, my physique was impressive; yes, I won the show with a perfect score. But I was lacking that ideal crispness and fullness of muscle mass. The reason was obvious: I'd miscalculated my carbohydrate intake just prior to the contest. I'll discuss this process of carbohydrate depletion and reloading in the chapter on diet. For now, let's just say this mishap was part of my trial-and-error adventure. One week after the show my legs looked superb. I could not believe my eyes. Where did these striations come from? What happened? Again, I'd learned a valuable lesson (the hard way) and snagged another Sandow statuette as a reward for my efforts.

Arnold—no stranger to the top of the bodybuilding universe—and attorney Jim Lorimer ran this Olympia like clockwork. It was well organized and professionally promoted. Everyone had a wonderful time.

On the competitive side, my old training partner Rich Gaspari really came into his own in '86. He was in excellent shape and moved up a notch into second place. The guy was becoming a little pest. I dubbed him Rich "The Itch" because he would not go away. He wasn't supposed

Haney at the lineup for the 1991 Olympia: "This is my night to party. I'm going to strut my stuff—here it is!"

to have such superb genetics. In fact, I used to call him "Fat Boy" because he enjoyed devouring hamburgers at the Fatburger restaurant in Reseda, California. He hated that nickname. But Rich never ceased to amaze me; he could trim down in size in a flash and be ripped and ready for the show.

Final Results:

1) Lee Haney
2) Rich Gaspari
3) Mike Christian
4) Albert Beckles
5) Berry DeMey
6) Peter Hensel
7) Bertil Fox
8) Ron Love
9) John Terilli
10) Josef Grolmus

THE 1987 MR. OLYMPIA: GOTHENBERG, SWEDEN

A very freaky experience. The '87 Olympia took place on Halloween and I called it "Fright Night." What I planned to reveal at this show was going to be frightening. I had every intention of being in the best shape of my life. Not surprisingly, though, a bunch of weird things happened to mess with my mind.

First of all, my plane reservations got all screwed up and I was packed into economy class—sitting shoulder-to-shoulder like a sardine for nine hours. My good friend Gil Ruiz was there to keep my head together, calm me down. He got me to the hotel and started preparing my meals. But I knew he was having second thoughts. I could read his mind: *Maybe I like Lee too much! What am I doing in Sweden cooking chicken when I could could be at home with my family?*

Everything was cool until Tuesday night, one day before I was scheduled to start carbohydrate loading. I stared at my body in the mirror and freaked—all my muscle definition had vanished; it was a whole lot of flat nothing! My physique resembled a stick figure, not exactly the form of a Mr. Olympia. I asked Gil if he thought I should start carb loading one day early. This was his succinct reply: "Lee, please don't ask me a question like that. Do you think I want to be responsible for such a big decision?"

But Gil was the only one who'd consistently seen my body the week before a contest. He understood the effects of the carbohydrate depletion and reloading process. Together, we made the choice to start putting carbs back into my diet that evening, one day ahead of schedule.

It was a calculated risk, but one that paid off in victory. I peaked just in time for the show on Saturday night: My skin was tight, the definition and crispness—perfection. I hit the stage and, boom, it was not even close. Gaspari finished a distant second and Lee Labrada exploded onto the bodybuilding scene into third place.

Through all the ups and downs of this Olympia, the one thing that stood out was the special feeling I carried around with me from the birth of my son Josh, who decided to come into the world on September 6, 1987. My sense of pride and joy made the fourth Olympia title all the more meaningful.

Final Results:

1) Lee Haney
2) Rich Gaspari
3) Lee Labrada
4) Mike Christian
5) Robby Robinson
6) Berry DeMey
7) Albert Beckles
8) Eduardo Kawak
9) Ron Love
10) Mike Ashley

THE 1988 MR. OLYMPIA: LOS ANGELES

I loved this show. Finally, the Olympia returned home to Los Angeles, the true mecca for bodybuilding. This is where the Olympia belongs. And the contest was promoted as an actual sporting event. Jeff Everson, then editor of *Muscle & Fitness,* provided TV commentary, and the Universal Amphitheater was packed to the rafters. This was what bodybuilding was all about: The last word on who was the best in a major international sport.

Los Angeles was the perfect setting. The beautiful Southern California sunshine created the ideal environment for pre-contest tanning, a very important variable in the world of bodybuilding; and I received support from the promoters, professionals who were sensitive to the needs of a bodybuilder in the days leading up to the show. That's a rarity.

Everything fell into place right on schedule and I peaked the night of the show. Carbohydrate depletion and reloading were no mystery to me anymore. No sweat. But one thing kept bothering me—my legs would only get cut at the very last minute. God, what was going wrong? I'll touch on this again in the section on the '91 Olympia.

As to the competition. Gaspari finished second again, DeMey moved up into third with a fresh posing routine, and Mohammed Benaziza came out of the woodwork to make a statement. That little guy was incredible: He had muscle definition all over the place. A new era was beginning, but I was still supreme.

Final Results:

1) Lee Haney
2) Rich Gaspari
3) Berry DeMey
4) Lee Labrada
5) Gary Strydom
6) Mike Quinn
7) Brian Buchanan
8) Samir Bannout
9) Ron Love
10) Bob Paris

THE 1989 OLYMPIA: RIMINI, ITALY

The most confusing, disorganized show I've ever been to in my life! Everything was screwed up from the very start. A brief recap on this fiasco: I'd tried to contact the sponsors before I left the United States. No response. Nothing. I decided to make my own travel arrangements with an equipment company called Techno-Gym. They did everything right—I was met at the airport and whisked away to a first-class hotel in a limousine. Nice hotel. The best food. Perfect.

Unfortunately, I later found out that Techno-Gym was a competitor to one of the Olympia's primary sponsors. Big headache. Big trouble. And all because the promoters never responded to my inquiries.

Things kept getting worse. On the day before the contest I was ordered to leave Rimini and take a three-hour drive to Milan for a ten-minute interview. I told the sponsors to forget it. What about my contest

Haney with two of the up-and-coming young bodybuilders, Shawn Ray (left) and Vince Taylor.

preparations? I'm supposed to blow off my diet, leave my family, and for what? I was frustrated, feeling stressed. This is not the way it's meant to be; when you're preparing for a show this kind of outside pressure cannot be tolerated. Believe me, it can hamper your progress; force your adrenal glands to do freaky things like flood over so your muscles look smooth and flat.

I was not at my best for this contest. Instead of hitting the stage at 247–250 pounds, I was up to 257—my heaviest weight for an Olympia! The symmetry was on target, thank heaven, but I lacked the sharp definition, the awesome cuts.

Yeah, I won my sixth title, but it wasn't easy. I had to pose my tail off. Comparison after comparison—that was never the case in the past. Winning gets harder every year. The judges expect more of your physique. And the rumors start to fly: "Haney didn't do this; Haney didn't do that." The judges hear this nonsense, but they only know one side of the story.

The real nightmare began shortly after the Olympia ended. The sponsors had planned a post-competition party for the athletes, but that was cancelled for lack of time. All the bodybuilders (with the exception of yours truly, who'd taken much criticism for making his own arrangements) were forced to leave Rimini at 4 A.M. to catch a train to Milan, where they were scheduled to leave on an early-morning flight. Well, they missed the flight. The next plane didn't depart for another four hours. Sure enough, the guys started fighting with each other. Treat athletes like a herd of cattle and what can you expect?

Now when athletes are fighting with each other I think it's safe to say that something is amiss. I don't fault Ben Weider, the head of the IFBB, for this situation. He responds immediately and professionally to any problems. But he can't oversee everything.

We need a new dialogue to set the tone for the future of bodybuilding, an agenda for treating the athletes with respect and dignity. In the old days, the seventies and early eighties, the bodybuilders were like a big happy family, joking and caring for each other. It was magic. The current generation will not get to experience that feeling of camaraderie unless something changes. I'm thankful I caught the tail end of that special era.

Battle of the awesome backs: Lee and Dorian Yates square off in double biceps from behind.

Final Results:

1) Lee Haney
2) Lee Labrada
3) Vince Taylor
4) Rich Gaspari
5) Mohammed Benaziza
6) Mike Christian
7) Mike Quinn
8) Brian Buchanan
9) Samir Bannout
10) Ron Love

THE 1990 MR. OLYMPIA: CHICAGO

I tied Arnold's record for total Olympia titles (seven) and set the new record for consecutive triumphs. And remember that I'd taken time away from my training to work with Evander Holyfield, who knocked out Buster Douglas for the heavyweight championship. I'd fulfulled two important goals for 1990, but something was missing.

Another view on triceps—Lee and Dorian go face to face.

That *something* was my total conditioning level—yes, it was off that year. I'd spread myself too thin. I wasn't quite up to par. But who was in top shape at the '90 show? Of course, Lee Labrada was getting a big push from the media. It didn't faze me a bit, though. I simply made an adjustment that destroyed his chances. Let me explain: Labrada was—and still is—fond of a ballerina-type posing style, very graceful and poetic. That's all he would show the judges. Frankly, I get pretty bored with that stuff.

So this is what I did: I decided to put together a posing routine that would destroy him: A tough, powerful presentation to the theme of "Looking Out For Number One." The posing amplified my size advantage over Labrada, and that was the clincher; I ate him up alive on stage.

Remember the '90 Olympia; it was very significant. I proved that superior posing, knowing how to accentuate your strengths, can overcome less-than-perfect conditioning. Know how to adjust your posing to suit your physique. We'll talk more about this in the chapter on posing.

Final Results:

1) Lee Haney
2) Lee Labrada
3) Shawn Ray
4) Mike Christian
5) Rich Gaspari
6) Francis Benfatto
7) Frank Hildebrand
8) Samir Bannout
9) Andreas Munzer
10) Eddie Robinson

THE 1991 MR. OLYMPIA: ORLANDO, FLORIDA

The year that I shattered Arnold's record and entered the history books. Now I was the Mohammed Ali of bodybuilding, there could be no doubt. But I heard plenty of doubts expressed in the media after the Olympia in Chicago. People questioned whether I deserved to win the title—and that really upset me.

I'm either a popular champion or no champion at all. I don't want to hear people saying, "He wasn't at his best; they just handed him the

The '91 posedown: "When I pulled off my shirt it was over—all over."

title; I'm tired of looking at Lee Haney." No way I'm going to sit back and accept being less than my best.

So I had some serious soul searching ahead of me. Should I come back for Number Eight, or should I retire with Seven? I asked my wife, Shirley, for her advice and she didn't even hesitate: "You have to go for Number Eight; you're too close to the record to stop now—don't even think about it."

Now the spiritual side of me took over. You receive according to your faith; if you don't have faith that you're going to achieve your goal, if it's not your real desire, then forget it—success will elude you throughout your life. I made up my mind that, yes, I'm going all out—I'm not leaving anything half-done.

I was under incredible pressure that entire year leading up to the show. Some people in the media were still pushing Lee Labrada as the real winner in Chicago. I'd signed a contract with TwinLab (a supplement company in competition with Weider—Ben Weider is the head

Joe Weider acknowledges the breaking of Arnold's record at the '91 Olympia.

Lee and family after the victory.

of the IFBB and Joe Weider is the man behind the Mr. Olympia contest), and my advisers were telling me I might not get a fair shake from the judges.

I didn't want to go down in history as the guy who won seven Mr. Olympias and blew it the eighth time around. My training and diet had to be perfect—nothing could be left to chance.

After training steadily for almost a year I knew I was ready to rock and roll. Before the show I heard some of the other bodybuilders talking about how they'd gained weight in the off-season, that they were big enough to compete with Lee Haney. Well, that just proved they hadn't learned anything from experience. You don't get big since I'm the biggest guy on stage. Work for more definition, take what God has given you and make it better.

When I pulled off my shirt it was over—all over. The standing ovation from the crowd told the whole story; it made me feel like a champion again.

And my performance dismissed all those doubts about politics changing the outcome of the Olympia. It proved that the IFBB—Ben Weider, Joe Weider, and the various judges—was an organization with men and women of integrity, honor, and dignity. They did the right thing; the man who deserved to win prevailed.

Final Results:

 1) Lee Haney
 2) Dorian Yates
 3) Vince Taylor
 4) Lee Labrada
 5) Shawn Ray
 6) Sonny Schmidt
 7) Francis Benfatto
 8) Thierry Pastel
 9) Achim Albrecht
10) Rich Gaspari

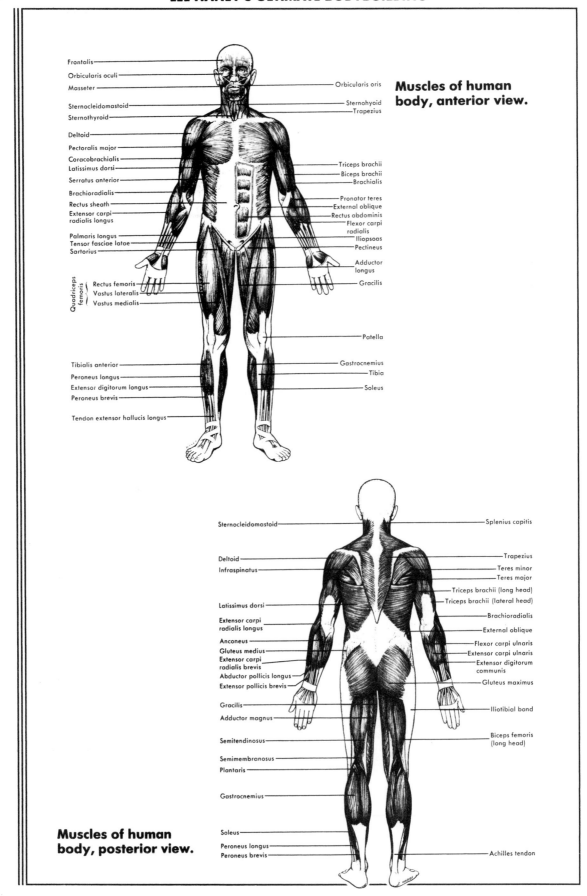

Frontalis
Orbicularis oculi
Masseter
Sternocleidomastoid
Sternothyroid
Deltoid
Pectoralis major
Coracobrachialis
Latissimus dorsi
Serratus anterior
Brachioradialis
Rectus sheath
Extensor carpi radialis longus
Palmaris longus
Tensor fasciae latae
Sartorius
Quadriceps femoris
Rectus femoris
Vastus lateralis
Vastus medialis
Tibialis anterior
Peroneus longus
Extensor digitorum longus
Peroneus brevis
Tendon extensor hallucis longus

Orbicularis oris
Sternohyoid
Trapezius
Triceps brachii
Biceps brachii
Brachialis
Pronator teres
External oblique
Rectus abdominis
Flexor carpi radialis
Iliopsoas
Pectineus
Adductor longus
Gracilis
Patella
Gastrocnemius
Tibia
Soleus

Muscles of human body, anterior view.

Sternocleidomastoid
Deltoid
Infraspinatus
Latissimus dorsi
Extensor carpi radialis longus
Anconeus
Gluteus medius
Extensor carpi radialis brevis
Abductor pollicis longus
Extensor pollicis brevis
Gracilis
Adductor magnus
Semitendinosus
Semimembranosus
Plantaris
Gastrocnemius
Soleus
Peroneus longus
Peroneus brevis

Splenius capitis
Trapezius
Teres minor
Teres major
Triceps brachii (long head)
Triceps brachii (lateral head)
Brachioradialis
External oblique
Flexor carpi ulnaris
Extensor carpi ulnaris
Extensor digitorum communis
Gluteus maximus
Iliotibial band
Biceps femoris (long head)
Achilles tendon

Muscles of human body, posterior view.

3

BUILDING YOUR FOUNDATION

No one can move right to an advanced program in any sport or discipline. Do you think I was knocking out 500-pound squats on my first foray into the gym? All bodybuilders and athletes must begin with a basic program. Two exercises per bodypart. A quick, effective forty-five minute workout. The beauty of this system is that it will sew the seeds for advanced development—if you intend to pursue a career in bodybuilding—or simply familiarize your body with the wonders of lifting weights.

All weight training springs from a careful analysis of your anatomy. What is a lat? What is a trap? Where are your deltoids? Study the anatomy chart I've provided (see page 24). Read journals on human movement. Get to know the exercises. Learn how to perform them correctly.

My foundation-building weight workout is amazingly easy. We're going to do the basic movements, the bread and butter of resistance training.

CHEST

Begin with an exercise that builds strength and size. I'm talking about the barbell bench press. It's a staple, one that will increase the muscle mass of your pecs, both pectoralis minor and major. The first time around you just want to learn how to control the weight. Start light and work your way up. Pyramid the weight, moving slowly up to higher poundages. Now that the chest is warm, hit the upper pecs with the incline barbell bench press. Don't try to become Mr. Olympia on your initial lift. Keep it light until you're warmed up. Be cool. Don't risk an injury for the sake of your ego.

    Bench press: 4 sets, 6–8 reps (the first is a warm-up)
    Incline bench press: 4 sets, 6–8 reps (including warm-up)

Barbell bench press: Lie back on a flat bench with a loaded barbell resting on a rack. The barbell should be positioned straight over your chest at arm's length. Reach up and grab the bar with an overhand grip, just beyond shoulder width. Inhaling, slowly lower the bar to mid-chest level; keep your arms outward and away from your chest. Exhaling, push the weight back up with all your strength, locking your elbows when it is as high as it will go.

Incline barbell bench press: **Performed in much the same way as a standard barbell bench press. Lie back on an incline bench positioned under a rack. I like to adjust the incline to a 30 degree angle—this is the perfect alignment to maximize upper pectoral muscle growth. Lift the bar off the rack, hold at arm's length above you, and lower it to your upper chest. Slowly return to the starting position and repeat.**

BACK

Stay basic. Kick things off with wide-grip pulldowns, either to the front or the back. Both variations are effective; select the version that's most comfortable. This is a rhythmic movement, one that develops quality and shape. Go with a weight you can handle. Think your way through the exercise, focusing on your lats. Feel the stretch as you bring the bar back up to the top.

Now advance to an explosive exercise, the barbell bent-over row. Use a light weight for the first set and pyramid to slowly and steadily increase resistance. Bent-over rows are the cornerstone of every intelligent back program. You cannot add size without them.

Wide-grip pulldown: 3–4 sets, 8–10 reps
Barbell bent-over row: 3–4 sets, 8–10 reps

Wide-grip pulldown: Sit at a pulldown station. Hold the bar with a wide grip. Pull the bar straight down to upper chest level; return to the starting position for the stretch.

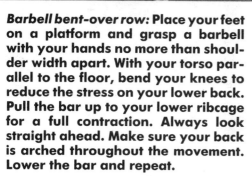

Barbell bent-over row: Place your feet on a platform and grasp a barbell with your hands no more than shoulder width apart. With your torso parallel to the floor, bend your knees to reduce the stress on your lower back. Pull the bar up to your lower ribcage for a full contraction. Always look straight ahead. Make sure your back is arched throughout the movement. Lower the bar and repeat.

Front military press (barbell): Sit at a bench positioned beneath a rack. Raise the bar to your shoulders; hands are placed slightly beyond shoulder width; feet are placed firmly on the floor. Press the bar to arm's length overhead, focusing tension on the front deltoids. Lower to the starting position and repeat.

SHOULDERS

Don't risk an injury with heavy lifts. Shoulder exercise is a tricky business. Avoid behind-the-neck military press for the first month or two; the position is a little awkward. I see some beginners lunging forward, grimacing in pain. Why take chances? Open with front shoulder presses (with a bar), an explosive movement that targets your front deltoid muscles. Then advance to lateral raises with light dumbbells, a rhythmic exercise that targets your medial (side) delts. Don't overkill. Two exercises are fine for beginners.

Military press: 3–4 sets, 8–10 reps
Lateral raise: 2–3 sets, 10–12 reps

Lateral raise (dumbbell): **Stand holding two dumbbells in front of you, palms facing each other. Raise the dumbbells in a semicircular motion until they reach shoulder height; pause, then return to the starting position along the same arc.**

BICEPS

A muscle that readily responds to stimulation. Just go with barbell curls (explosive) and preacher curls (rhythmic). The bar curls add size; the preacher curls enhance definition. Every now and then it's okay to add a set or two of concentration curls to force more blood into the peak of the biceps.

Barbell curl: 4 sets, 6–8 reps
Preacher curl: 3–4 sets, 10–12 reps

Barbell curl: Grasp the bar with a slightly wider than shoulder-width grip. Begin with the bar resting at your thighs, then curl it up to just below your chin. Keep your elbows close to your torso throughout the movement, and do not lock-out at the bottom of the curl. Keep your arms slightly bent at the bottom; this will ease the tension on your joints and demand more work from your biceps.

Preacher curl: **Adjust a preacher bench so that the top side is even with your ribcage. Place your arms downward across the bench and lean over it—the bench supports at triceps level. Using a shoulder-width, palms-up grip, curl the barbell in an upward arc until your biceps are fully contracted, while keeping your upper arms on the bench. Only your elbows and forearms move during the exercise. Lower and repeat.**

Concentration curl: Sit on a bench with a dumbbell in your left hand; your right hand is resting on your right knee for support. *Starting phase:* Your left arm is fully extended. *Middle phase:* Curl the weight up for a half movement, forcing blood into the biceps. *Final phase:* Curl the dumbbell up to your left shoulder to blast the peak of the biceps. Lower and repeat for the same number of reps on your right arm.

TRICEPS

Warm-up with triceps pressdowns. Stick with a light weight. Then get serious (lift a tad heavier) when performing the lying-down triceps extensions. These two exercises will suffice. If you don't have access to a pressdown machine, just do lying extensions or one-arm dumbbell extensions. One exercise—done correctly—is all you need to get started.

Triceps pressdown: 4 sets, 10–12 reps
Lying-down triceps extension: 3–4 sets, 8–10 reps

Triceps pressdown: Grasp the bar at a triceps pressdown station with a palms-down grip. Slowly press the bar down and keep your arms close in to your sides so that only your forearms—not your elbows—are moving. Use as heavy a weight as you can handle. Return to the starting position and repeat.

Lying triceps extension: **Lie back on a flat bench, holding an EZ-curl bar with your hands in a close grip. Press the bar up until your arms are almost locked out (fully extended). Keeping your elbows in place, lower the bar to your forehead, contracting your triceps, and press back up to the starting position. Never bend your wrists during the movement.**

CALVES

Don't go crazy with tons of exercises. Just do standing toe raises, pyramiding from a moderate to a heavy weight. Raise your toes as high as possible, pause, then return to the starting position—the balls of your feet rest on a foot pad, two-by-four, or an elevated block.

Standing toe raise: 4–5 sets, 20 reps

ABDOMINALS

Do your incline sit-ups—crunching your ribcage and pelvis as close together as possible—and seated leg crunches, which place minimal strain on your lower back. Simplicity is the key. Don't overcomplicate your workouts while you're in the process of getting into shape.

Incline sit-up: 3–4 sets, 15–20 reps
Seated crunch: 3–4 sets, 15–20 reps

Incline sit-up: **Opt for the small incline chair (as in the photo) and secure your feet under the pads. Bend your elbows and crunch forward, bringing your elbows toward your knees. Exhale on the contraction.**

Seated leg raise: Sit at the end of a bench; your hands are parallel to your upper thighs to ensure balance. Starting phase: Your legs are extended out in front of you. Now lean back slightly and raise your knees up—and in closer to your chest—while keeping them bent. Hold the position, then slowly lower your legs until they're fully extended.

LEGS

Nice and easy. The 45-degree leg press for explosive strength; leg extensions (a rhythmic movement) for quality; leg curls to tone and strengthen your hamstrings. Avoid squats in the first month of leg training. If you're really champing at the bit to start squatting, then flip-flop squats with leg presses. But learn the correct execution (see photo and caption), wear a belt to protect your lower back, and commence training with a weight you can control. Get in touch with the feel of the weight. Squats will make you or break you—and by "break you" I mean that you'll be injured.

Leg extension: 3–4 sets, 12–15 reps
45-degree leg press: 4 sets, 10–12 reps
Leg curl: 3–4 sets, 12–15 reps

Leg extension: Sit in a leg-extension machine set, your feet hooked under the pads. Extend your legs out as far as possible, flex your thighs, and slowly lower the weight just short of the starting position. Don't let the weight drop; you want to keep continual pressure on your quads.

Squat: Note that I'm ready for safe lifting: I'm wearing a weight belt and have my knees wrapped up for an extra measure of protection. When doing squats I use two foot positions—a shoulder-width stance, allowing me to work inner thigh and hamstring, and a narrower stance for stressing outer and front quadriceps. Use strict form in both cases. Step under a barbell that's positioned on a rack (or one of the many machines used for this purpose, as in the photo), and let it rest across the backs of your shoulders. Holding onto the bar to balance it, raise it off the rack as you step back into the starting position. Now lower your body into the full squat; execute the movement with your feet flat on the floor, back upright and head up. Come down to the bottom, then propel yourself back up to the starting phase, making sure you do not lose control of the weight.

45-degree leg press: **Recline on a 45-degree leg press; your hips should be directly below the weights. As with squats, you can vary your foot placement; shoulder-width apart is the most common alignment. Make sure your feet are firmly in place before starting your lift. Straighten the legs and push the weight upward, then slowly lower it as deep as you can. Push the weight back up the starting position.**

Leg curl: Lie facedown on a leg-curl machine, with your heels locked under the pads of the lever mechanism. Grasp the handles on the front of the bench for support. Then curl the weight up towards your buttocks. Bring your feet as far back as you can—feel the contraction in your hamstrings, then lower the weight. Tips on form: Your hips stay on the bench at all times. Stretch your hamstrings at the end of each set.

This is a very quick workout. You can pop in the gym—bam, bam, bam—and be done in less than forty-five minutes. No fooling around. No socializing with friends. Take care of business and get out. Since the workout is so brief, you can train six days a week—three days on, one day off—without getting injured or burned out.

THE SCHEDULE

Day 1: Biceps/Chest/Abdominals
Day 2: Shoulders/Back
Day 3: Triceps/Legs/Abdominals

Take a day off and repeat the cycle in sequence.

If you only have time to lift three days a week, then try this format:

Monday: Upper Body
Wednesday: Lower Body
Friday: Upper Body

Switch the order around the following week so that you're working lower body twice, every other cycle.

Do your aerobic (cardiovascular) exercise—at least three days a week, twenty minutes per session, at 65–85 percent of your maximum heart rate (MHR)—after your weight workout. Your MHR is calculated by subtracting your age from 220. If you're thirty-two—as I am—then your MHR is 188 beats per minute. Avoid aerobic training on leg day; it's overkill for the quadriceps and hamstrings.

I'm serious! This is the ideal stratagem for integrating training into your lifestyle. You don't want to work out intensely for a month or two, then shine it on like a fad or trend. No. Building an impressive physique demands consistency and dedication.

PARTNER TRAINING

Just starting out? Ripped to pieces after years of lifting? Either way, partner training is an excellent workout option. A partner can assist you with forced reps, allowing you to hoist those heavy weights you can't handle on your own. He or she can also provide motivation and camaraderie. It's a special feeling, sharing goals and working as a team to transcend limits of strength and endurance.

Selecting a partner isn't easy. Here are a few things to consider: Find a person who is as serious as you are. Totally committed. Unselfish to the core. If you need a spotter and your partner is too busy checking out

Selecting the right training partner can really improve your results.

the action in the corner, then I recommend finding a new collaborator.

Never become too dependent on your partner. What if he feels like crap? That negative energy can spill over into your workout. Be wary of this scenario: "I'm not up for training today. Let's go have a burger. Lucy was terrible last night. I'm going to get a divorce." He's ready to shoot himself and you're somehow supposed to enjoy doing bench presses. No way. Don't let a partner drag you down; the idea is to get motivated—not disillusioned—by your buddy.

I like partners who share my love for training. No distractions. We just rock and roll. And, yes, we have a ball. We laugh. We bust each other's butts. I know he wants me to do that extra rep. I don't have to

tell him, "Why are you looking around the room?" I better not have to say that to my partner. If I do, then he's not going to be my partner for long.

Screen your partners carefully—that's what I do. Feel comfortable with the person from day one. Rick Gianone, a trusted ally and true friend, is a perfect example. Rick trained with me back in 1984 when I won my first Olympia. He's six-feet-two-inches, 310 pounds, and he curls 225 and benches 500. Rick believes in using heavy weights and I do my best to keep up with him. We complement each other. He pushes me to new extremes. That's why I brought him back to train with me for the '91 Olympia.

Tyrone "Ropeman" Felder is totally crazy, a prerequisite for being one of my training partners. He turns his hat around to the back—the way a lot of young kids do these days—and I know he's ready to move. Then there's "Superman," a great guy to have on your side in the gym. I remember one training session in particular: We were matching each other set for set, rep for rep. I looked back at him and sweat was streaming down his face. Man, he was so intense. I like that. Now that's

what I call a motivator. He was one of the first people to suggest I could break Arnold's record—way back in 1985—and it really made an impression on me. It inspired a higher level of achievement.

Select someone who cares about making progress as much as you do. Fred Richards, a retired Marine and a great friend who trained with me for the 1990 Olympia, would say: "You are what you eat and you are the company you keep." Negativity breeds negativity. Positive energy brings out the best in people. Train with a person who believes in you. It can't work any other way.

SAFETY AND COMMON SENSE

Never take anything for granted in the gym. Anticipate what could go wrong. Consider the safety of the people working out in your vicinity. Even experienced lifters make mistakes. One of my training partners broke a toe once because he wasn't applying common sense to his workout strategy. After a set of pullovers, he absentmindedly left the dumbbell dangling off the edge of the flat bench, an accident waiting to happen. Sure enough, he gets back to the bench and the dumbbell plops down on his foot—gotcha! The weight broke his toe in one fell swoop.

This accident could have been prevented with a little common sense. Here are a few simple tips:

- Never rest dumbbells on a bench.
- Always use safety collars to ensure that the plates don't slip off and cause an injury—either to you or anyone else. This applies to squats, curls, or any exercises relying on a barbell or dumbbell.
- Use weight belts, straps, and gloves to support heavy lifts. Mother Nature did not intend for you to lug 200 pounds on your back. Wear a belt to protect the lumbar region of your spine. Put on knee wraps for heavy squats to support the integrity of your tendons and ligaments.
- Don't take unnecessary chances. The last thing you want to do is rupture a disc or injure your lower back. Once you screw up your lower back, well, it's a chronic condition. Low back injuries haunt you for life. So train safe. Always control the weight; never allow the weight to control you.

   This isn't just a two- or four-year experiment. I want you to enjoy training for a lifetime. Look at Albert Beckles, one of

BUILDING YOUR FOUNDATION

EXERCISE	SETS	REPS
CHEST		
Bench press	4*	6–8
Incline bench press	4*	6–8
*first set is a warm-up		
BACK		
Wide-grip pulldown	3–4	8–10
Barbell bent-over row	3–4	8–10
SHOULDERS		
Military press	3–4	8–10
Lateral raise	2–3	10–12
BICEPS		
Barbell curl	4	6–8
Preacher curl	3–4	10–12
TRICEPS		
Triceps pressdown	4	10–12
Lying triceps extension	3–4	8–10
CALVES		
Standing toe raise	4–5	20
ABDOMINALS		
Incline sit-up	3–4	15–20
Seated crunch	3–4	15–20
LEGS		
Leg extension	3–4	12–15
45 degree leg press	4	10–12
Leg curl	3–4	12–15

the most respected bodybuilders in the world. He's past sixty and is still in amazing physical condition. What a physique! He's ageless. I wouldn't mind being as ripped as Albert when I'm his age.

■ Don't whip a tired horse! The easiest road to injury is training when you're lightheaded, sleep-deprived, or low on glycogen because of improper diet. Go home and get some rest. Enjoy a medium-protein, high complex carbohydrate meal. Take your supplements (see chapter six). Now you can get back in the gym and kick some butt. Do the right thing. Don't abuse your body in the name of fitness. You can't be fit if you're walking around on crutches or hobbled with lower back pain. Your body is not dumb if you will let it be smart. I like that! Take care of your body and it will respond.

4

THE ULTIMATE WORKOUTS FOR ADVANCED BODYBUILDING

Now it's time to enter "The Animal Kingdom," the inner sanctum of my advanced training experience.

The Animal Kingdom is the name of my gym in Atlanta. It's a hardcore environment. No fooling around. No half-hearted reps. No nonsense. That's not to say I don't enjoy myself when I work out. I like to laugh and go crazy. But there's no substitute for focused training, entering into a zone of total connection between the mind and muscle. That's what the Animal Kingdom is all about—it's my adventureland in muscle-building, the perfect place for muscle expansion and stimulation.

My ultimate workout regimen took shape while I prepared for the 1991 Olympia. I had eight years of Olympia competition under my belt. I analyzed all my training programs to settle upon the most awesome combination of exercises. I picked the best workouts from each year to find out what made me freaky (big and impressive in size and striations), and the bodypart sessions that would bring out that vibrant muscle mass.

The secret formula for success is quite simple: Use a combination of explosive movements and rhythmic movements to hit each bodypart. The explosive movements stimulate development of the white muscle cells; the rhythmic movements stimulate development of the red muscle cells. This is a modern, high-tech method that allows you to understand the principles of muscle growth and how they relate to various bodybuilding exercises.

Advanced bodybuilding is divided into three phases of intensity, each with a different period of recovery. Phase 3 is the most intense; Phase 2 is the intermediate level; and Phase 1 is the least taxing of the workouts. With some bodyparts—legs, for instance—phases 1 and 2 are comparable in intensity; the distinction is more a matter of your particular training objective—Phase 1 builds mass, Phase 2 increases definition.

Let's go through my advanced program, bodypart by bodypart, to put you on the road to a better physique. You'll note that not all bodyparts have three phases of intensity (calves, for instance) nor do all move strictly from an explosive to a rhythmic movement. Nothing is written in stone. Everything in my system is based on personal experience, striving for the simplest possible solutions to training problems. If it works, fine. If it doesn't, just forget it. Build up your muscles without tearing down your body. Why reinvent the wheel, anyway? Let's work with the basic framework to find success.

SECTION 1: HANEY'S LEGS

God, why do my legs wait until the last two days before a show to get cut and defined? My attitude was always, *Hey, I want my legs to get extra ripped; I'll do every exercise under the sun to ensure peak performance*—squats, leg presses, hack squats, sissy squats, lunges, leg extensions, leg curls, stiff-legged deadlifts, single-leg curls. *I'm not going to miss out on any exercise!*

This do-it-all-in-one-workout approach gave me nothing but grief— my legs never came in until the last minute. I kept thinking, *I had these freaky, ripped legs at the Teenage Nationals.* And in 1986, when I did fewer exercises per workout, my legs were ripped to pieces. The cuts came in on time—no problem.

It finally dawned on me that I was overtraining my legs. In trying to stimulate muscle growth, I was annihilating my poor muscles. There's no need to torture your legs; just do the right thing and they will respond.

Phase 1: The Mass Builder

This is an off-season program for building meat—muscle size and power. Start performing the exercises at least three to six months before a major competition.

Always begin with leg extensions—they bring out the striations in your thigh (quadriceps) muscles. Leg extensions are also the perfect warm-up movement. In the past, I'd start my leg workout with squats. Not so smart; that was a great way to torment my knees. But back in 1984 I did not have a clue on how to train scientifically—I was winging it. I wanted to pump up my legs in the first ten minutes of training. Don't rush your workout. Take the time you need to warm up your muscles for optimal gains in size and quality.

Leg extensions: 5 sets, 12–15 reps

Leg presses are next on the agenda. Even after leg extensions, the knees are not ready to handle those heavy squats. Either the vertical leg press or the more standard 45-degree leg press will do the job. The vertical leg press is my personal preference; you get a better feel for the movement. Unfortunately, many gyms no longer have this equipment—it's a throwback to the *Pumping Iron* era when training was bad to the bone.

Leg presses: 4–5 sets, 8–10 reps

Time to move onto heavy squats. Your legs are warmed up. They're aching for the ultimate size-builder. Do not expect to lift as much weight as you normally would, though, as your quadriceps are somewhat fatigued from the leg extensions and leg presses. No wonder; on all of these exercises you're going to pyramid the weight—use progressively heavier poundages with each successive set. Start light and work your way up. Allow the muscle to adjust to the forces of resistance.

I do not believe in descending sets—the down side of the pyramid where you suddenly decrease the weight. I may occasionally do a descending set on leg extensions if I want to really shock the muscle. But that's unusual.

Building muscle size is a simple matter of supply and demand. No need for a grasp of economic theory, thankfully; just consider this basic rule: Supply more intensity (weight) to the muscle and it will demand progressively heavier weights for added growth. This is why your body adapts to the same type of stimulation, and why you must vary your program as much as possible by going up in weight as strength allows.

Adapt to the resistance, then move on to the next level. That's what the Pyramid Principle is all about.

If you can usually squat 400 pounds, don't expect to lift more than 300 on this program. Work your way up to the top of the pyramid. Three hundred pounds will feel like a ton after all those leg extensions and leg presses.

Squats: 4–5 sets, 8–10 reps

That's it for the frontal thigh on my mass-builder. I'll come back that evening and do leg curls and stiff-legged deadlifts for hamstrings. Weight stays fairly heavy.

Leg curls: 4–5 sets, 8–10 reps
Stiff-legged deadlifts: 4–5 sets, 8–10 reps

Stiff-legged deadlift: Stand on an elevated block or low flat bench and place a barbell in front of your feet. Hold the bar—palms down—with your hands roughly 14 to 16 inches apart. Bend at the waist with your head up, back straight and knees locked. Now straighten up until the bar reaches upper thigh level. Focus on your hamstrings and lower back while lifting the weight, then return to the starting position.

HANEY'S LEGS

WORKOUT #1: THE MASS BUILDER

EXERCISE	SETS	REPS
Leg extension	5	12–15
45 degree or Vertical leg press	4–5	8–10
Squat	4–5	6–8 or 8–10
Hamstrings in the evening		
Leg curl	4–5	8–10
Stiff-legged deadlift	3–5	8–10

WORKOUT #2: THE QUALITY (DEFINITION) BUILDER

EXERCISE	SETS	REPS
Leg extension	3	10–12
45 degree or Vertical leg press	5	10–12
Hack squat	5	12–15
Hamstrings in the evening		
Single leg curl or leg curl	4–5	8–10
Stiff-legged deadlift	3–4	8–10

Continued on next page

WORKOUT #3: THE FREAKOUT

EXERCISE	SETS	REPS
Leg extension	5	12–15
45 degree or Vertical leg press	5	8–10
Squat	4–5	6–8
Hack squat	5	12–15

Hamstrings in the evening

Leg curl	4–5	8–10
Stiff-legged deadlift	3–4	8–10

WORKOUT #4: (THE LAST 7 WEEKS BEFORE THE CONTEST)

EXERCISE	SETS	REPS
Leg extension	5–7	15–20
Leg press	5	12–15
Hack squat	4–5	12–15
Lunge*	3–4	15 (per leg)
Sissy squat*	4	15

Every other workout: Superset (alternate exercises with little or no rest between sets) leg extensions (4 sets, 15–20 reps) and hack squats (4–5 sets, 12–15 reps) at the end of the leg workout.

*Do one or the other.

Phase 2: The Quality Builder

This a very intense workout, one that places more emphasis on definition than size. Alternate this with Phase 1, taking three days off between leg workouts. High-intensity training demands a minimal amount of recovery time after each set. Pause for thirty-five seconds and move on. It's a quick—bam, bam, bam—and effective strategy for carving out new cuts in the muscle.

Start with three sets of leg extensions (10–12 reps) to warm up the knees. Then begin the routine in earnest with leg presses; in this workout you will not perform squats. Leg presses allow you to develop a feel for working the muscle without worrying as much about balance, a major concern when you're squatting heavy poundages. Just flex and squeeze your thigh at the top, focusing all your energy on linking the mind and muscle together.

Though the 45-degree leg press is more than adequate, I really want you to seek out a vertical leg press (also known as a wide-stance leg press on a wall-type leg press machine). When you compare the 45-degree to the vertical it's a different world. Comparatively speaking, you're on a picnic with the 45-degree leg press. You can converse with your friends: "Hey, Bill, how's it going?" But with the vertical leg press it's more like: "Help me, Bill!"

Okay, don't get intimidated. It's really not that bad. I want to explain the precise vertical leg press technique so that you'll get it straight:

Lie on the support pad under the vertical leg press machine. Place your hips directly under the foot pad. Now place your feet on the pad, about sixteen- to twenty-inches apart. Push the rack holding the weight up until your legs are fully extended, with your knees locked out. Remove the safety clips and rest your hands under your butt, palms down. Now lower the rack and bring your knees down toward your rib cage, but don't come too far down or you can injure yourself. Always keep a certain amount of tension in your legs, especially on the descent. Make sure your knees fan out and your hips are down, then push back up to the starting position.

Proper breathing is essential. Never hold your breath; the same rule applies to the squat. I exhale as the legs descend toward my rib cage and inhale on the way back up. Switch it around and you'll get dizzy.

Leg presses: 5 sets, 10–12 reps

Now go back to your trusty hack squats, another quality builder. Hacks do not, however, build as much mass as the leg press; it's a

Hack squat: **When preparing to do hacks, be sure that the foot platform is angled so that your knees are not under extreme pressure. Also note that I'm wearing knee wraps for added protection. Now that you're ready to press forward, plant your feet slightly in front of the body. The stance should be at least 12½ inches wide. Lower the weight in a squatting position until the thighs are parallel to the ground, go down for a complete contraction (the last photo in the sequence), then press back up to the top until your thighs are fully extended.**

rhythmic movement designed for detailing the contours of the thigh.

It's such a simple exercise: Come down into the squat position with control and then thrust forward; push off on your heels (extending your feet outward) to bring more muscle fiber into play. Then, as you return to the top, squeeze and slowly flex your thigh muscles—never snap or jerk at the top or you can ruin your knees.

This is a very effective exercise and it doesn't require a lot of weight. I see some guys putting tons of weight on a hack machine. A hack isn't made for that; it's a quality—not a mass—builder. If you want to lift heavy, opt for squats or heavy leg presses.

Hack squats: 5 sets, 12–15 reps

Return to the gym that same evening to work your hamstrings.

Leg curls, Single leg curls: 4–5 sets, 8–10 reps
Stiff-legged deadlifts: 3–4 sets, 8–10 reps

The Phase 1 and Phase 2 leg sessions are my main off-season programs. I'm not overtraining the muscles. I'm giving the quadriceps and hamstrings enough recovery time—three days of rest between workouts—to bounce back fresh and ready for action. The bigger you are, the longer it takes to recover from a workout. It's not the quantity but the quality. Remember that saying whenever you train for a sport.

Moderation is all well and good. Every now and then, though, you want to shock the muscles. Believe me, the element of surprise is a handy training tactic. That's where my Phase 3 session, "The Freakout," picks up the slack. If I think my legs aren't responding, I do leg extensions, leg presses, squats and hack squats for frontal thigh; then I pop back into the gym that evening and kick out leg curls and stiff-legged deadlifts. Same sets and reps as in the other programs. Use this type of program every 1½ to 2 weeks.

Ten weeks before the Olympia I back away from the Phase 3 monster session. Seven weeks before the Olympia I get rid of the squats, too. The vertical leg press is more than enough. If you don't have a vertical leg press available to you, then continue to squat at least once a week. Don't overtrain at the last minute. If you haven't built up the size by that time, you might as well forget it. Stick to a reasonable, balanced approach as your competition draws near.

The Pre-Contest Formula

Kick back on the weight and pump up the repetitions. You want to really feel the burning sensation in the muscle, that awareness of increased endurance and stamina. Go for the pump, but be smart. Don't kill yourself—or your legs—to get a good workout.

This is what I do before the show:

    Leg extensions: 15–20 reps (as a warm-up)
    Vertical leg presses: 12–15 reps (to build a little more size)
    Hack squats: 15 reps (for quality)

then I add:

    Lunges: (holding two 35-pound dumbbells) or
    Sissy squats: (just using my own bodyweight for resistance) as
        a finishing movement.

Occasionally, just to keep life interesting, I'll superset hack squats and leg extensions at the end of the workout for a change of pace. The evening hamstring workout stays the same. If it isn't broken, why fix it?

The aforementioned leg routine is my exclusive training system, a can't-miss path to size and striations. It sure paid off for the '91 Olympia. Ten weeks before the show everything looked good. A week before the show I was ripped to pieces. No more begging: "Please, legs, please!" at the last minute. Finally, I discovered the perfect balance between hard work and common sense.

Lunge: **Place your lead foot (in the photo it's the left foot) on an elevated block. With a dumbbell in each hand—head up, back straight, feet about 5 inches apart—lunge forward with the left leg until your left thigh is almost parallel to the floor. Keep your right leg as straight as possible. Step back into the starting position and repeat on the right leg for the same number of reps.**

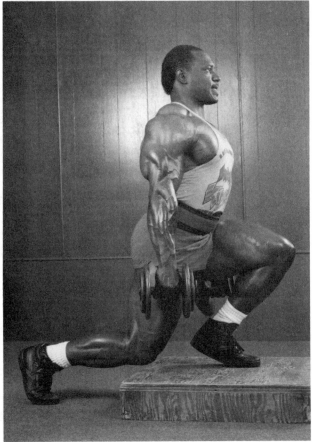

Sissy squat: Stand with your palms facing you, holding a bar supported on a rack. Take a close grip on the bar. Relying on the bar for support, squat while raising your toes, thrusting your hips forward and arching your back. Descend until your thighs are roughly parallel to the ground, or until you feel a full contraction in your quads, back arched and knees as close together as possible. Return to the starting position. All resistance is provided by your bodyweight.

SECTION 2: HANEY'S CALVES

Great calves—always the baby that everyone is after. I'm very conscious of my calf development. What choice do I have? Well-toned, symmetrical calves can make or break a physique up on stage—or on the beach, for that matter.

Your calf muscles (the soleus and gastrocnemius) walk around with you all day, every day. This constant wear and tear gives the calves resiliency—in other words they are very hard to stimulate. What can you do to wake up these jokers? Lift with very heavy weights, while using correct form on the three most effective exercises:

Calf Killer Number One: Standing Toe Raises

I like to do eight sets for 15–20 reps. Think of the first two sets as a warm-up. Then start packing on the weight until you burnout in the 15–20 range. I peak at about 500 pounds on the last set. Don't push your luck! Just lift a weight you handle for 15–20 reps, doing half movements on the last 5–7 reps as you approach muscle failure.

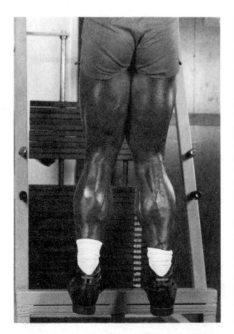 

Standing toe raise: **Stand with the weight on the machine leveraged under your shoulders. The balls of your feet must be positioned on a toe block. Lower your heels as far as possible, then straighten your body and rise up on your toes as high as you can.**

Calf Killer Number Two: Donkey Calf Raises

Same basic approach as the standing toe raise. Do these on a machine instead of the old-fashioned way—with a training partner riding on your back, always guaranteed to embarrass you in the gym.

Donkey calf raise: **Stand in a bent-over position under the lower back pad of the donkey-calf machine. Place your hands on the support handles in front of you. The balls of your feet should rest on the edge of the platform. Lower your heels as far down as possible, then rise up on your toes as high as you can go.**

Calf Killer Number Three: Seated Toe Raises

I turn to this detail developer—it accentuates the split between the gastrocnemius and the soleus—in the final twelve weeks before a contest. Do these slowly, squeeze the calf muscles, and focus on shaping that rounded sweep. Keep the weight and reps high; your calves can take it!

Seated toe raise: Seated on the bench of a calf machine, place the balls of your feet on the toe block and insert your knees under the machine bar. Then raise your toes, and—with your knees—push the machine's weight as far upward as possible. Resist the weight, then lower your heels as far below the level of the toes as possible. Stretch and repeat.

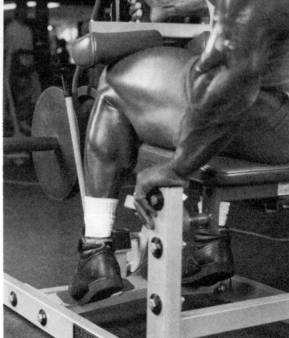

HANEY'S CALVES

EXERCISE	SETS	REPS
Standing toe raise*	8	15–20
Donkey calf raise*	8	15–20

Rest interval: two days between sessions.
Pre-Contest (7–10 weeks before a show)

*Do one or the other
per workout.

EXERCISE	SETS	REPS
Seated toe raise	8	15–20
Standing toe raise*	8	15–20
Donkey calf raise*	8	15–20

*Do one or the other
per workout.

One Final Word on Calves

Pointing your toes inward on calf exercise (to stimulate the growth of the outer part of the calf) is a sensible variation. Try doing a set or two this way for each of the three calf movements. Do not, however, turn your toes outward to stimulate the inner calf. A wide inner calf is one thing you don't have to worry about—it will develop without any extra emphasis in your workout. Stick with a practical approach to training. Don't fall prey to silly notions that are not based on empirical evidence.

SECTION 3: HANEY'S BICEPS

Master the illusion of size; in the case of your biceps, the peak creates the impression that your muscles are larger than life. Consider the physique of Lee Haney. My back and shoulders have always been really huge. When I turned to the side in my posing, though, my biceps got lost in the shuffle. Man, I had to do something to force those suckers to grow.

I had a lot on my mind leading up to the '91 Olympia. I was thinking about adding that extra half inch to my peak and remembered what Tom Platz—an accomplished bodybuilder in the 1970s and early 1980s—preached about half movements and forced reps: Allow a partner to assist you with the exercise. Take the execution halfway through a full range of motion. Now, using a heavier weight than you could lift by yourself, force as much blood into the muscle as possible. Do the half movement, go for the awesome pump that forces the muscle cell to split (stimulating substantial growth) at the end of the workout, and ease off on the contraction to allow the blood to flow out of that area.

It's amazingly simple: heavy weights, half movements, and total concentration translate into moving past the pain barrier—the pump that locks the blood into the head of the biceps, prodding the peak into important growth and muscle cell expansion.

The Phase 3 Biceps Workout: Pump Up the Volume

Hitting the peak is the X-factor in training biceps, but you cannot sacrifice the sheer size you get from doing barbell curls.

Barbell curls are the meat and potatoes of biceps training. They're comparable in importance to bench presses (chest), barbell rows and T-bar rows (back), military presses (shoulders) and squats (legs)—the basic explosive movements that build power and size by targeting the white muscle cell. All of these lifts rely on hoisting heavy weight in the 6–8 rep range. Do not be afraid to cheat a little to lift even heavier on the bar curls—cheating in this context does not give you a green light to screw around; it means you can put your back into the movement for the last two or three forced reps.

I designed the Phase 3 biceps routine to launch from an explosive movement to a rhythmic movement—the barbell preacher curl. It's a slow, controlled arc; squeeze at the top, pump blood into the muscle, then ease off. Your biceps are somewhat pre-exhausted after a set of barbell curls. Reps stay in the 10–12 range, typical for most rhythmic exercises.

After one set each of barbell and preacher curls, sink your teeth into a punishing set of concentration curls. Use a lighter weight, something that will allow you to really focus on the head of the biceps. If a training partner is handy, apply the half movement, forced rep principle to force even more blood into the peak. (See chapter 3 for photographs of these three curls.)

The Phase 3 routine features my special giant set stratagem: Perform one set of each movement with little or no rest between exercises. Then kick back for one minute, pause to refresh, and immediately repeat the set sequence four times:

Barbell curls: 6–8 reps
Preacher curls: 10–12 reps
Concentration curls: 10–12 reps

I guarantee that this workout will force your biceps to grow in a hurry. The muscle will plead for mercy: "Please, can't we do something else today?" But don't give in; you've got to punish that bodypart to stimulate gains in size and definition. Do not repeat this workout more than once every 1 ½ to two weeks. Sure, it's only three exercises, but the extreme intensity dictates considerable recovery time.

The Phase 2 Biceps Workout

Again, a very intense training regimen. Allow for three days between workouts. Perform the same exercises, sets and reps as in Phase 3; however, you're dropping the giant set in favor of a slower, more methodical approach. Complete your sets and reps for each exercise before moving on. And thanks to the added recovery time between sets—trust

Seated incline dumbbell curl: Lie on an incline bench with a dumbbell in each hand. Begin with the dumbbells at close to arm's length (down at thigh level). Curl the weights up past your upper thighs, then to shoulder height (for a full contraction); squeeze, then lower the dumbbells to the starting position and repeat.

HANEY'S BICEPS

PHASE 3 (HIGHEST INTENSITY)

EXERCISE	SETS	REPS
Barbell curl*	4–5	6–8
Preacher curl*	4–5	10–12
Concentration curl*	4–5	10–12

*Perform as a giant set; do
one set of each with little or no
rest in-between; pause for one
minute, then start again until
you've completed the second set.
Follow the same format for the
last two or three sets.

PHASE 2 (INTERMEDIATE INTENSITY)

EXERCISE	SETS	REPS
Barbell curl	5	6–8
Preacher curl	4	12
Concentration curl	3	12–15
Seated incline dumbbell curl	3	10–12

PHASE 1 (MODERATE INTENSITY)

EXERCISE	SETS	REPS
Barbell curl	4	6–8
Preacher curl	4	12–15
Concentration curl	3	8–10

me—you'll be able to squeeze out one more exercise: the infamous seated incline dumbbell curl. Align the bench as high as possible; this position allows you to pump more blood into the muscle on the contraction. Turn your palms straight up at the top; never allow the muscle to relax. Do 3 sets, 10–12 reps. This entire workout totals no more than 15 sets, even with the addition of the seated incline dumbbell curls.

The Phase 1 Biceps Workout

Almost too easy. I'll fall back on this routine after a long flight, when I'm recovering from a Phase 3 program, or if I'm burning out on training. The nice thing about it is you can bounce back and advance to Phase 2 or 3 after just two days of rest. It's a three-part process:

Barbell curls: 4 sets, 6–8 reps (for size)
Preacher curls: 4 sets, 12–15 reps (for shape and quality)
Concentration curls: 3 sets, 8–10 reps (for a bigger peak)

Explosive, rhythmic, then isolation. I'm offering you the best of three worlds.

SECTION 4: HANEY'S TRICEPS

Battle of the Triceps: The Ultimate Test of My Supremacy

Could I exceed Mike Christian's triceps in size, definition, and striations? The answer, of course, always came back an emphatic "yes!" Of course, Mike would disagree. Treat your triceps as the perfect showpiece for muscularity and definition; big arms never fail to impress the judges and your fellow competitors.

Working triceps is much like biceps—you must really feel what's going on inside the muscle. No need to knock out tons of movements. I prefer a shorter, more disciplined approach to the triceps training game.

The Two Basic Off-Season Workouts: Phase 2 and 3

All triceps sessions begin with the classic triceps pressdown, a movement that combines explosive and rhythmic exercise principles (see chapter

3). Explode at the top and squeeze—don't jerk or snap—at the bottom. It's so easy and basic, an excellent way to warm up the muscles for the rest of your workout. I usually stay in the 10–12 range; depending on how I feel, though, I might take the reps up a bit higher—12–15. It's an intuitive situation; you must know how much punishment the triceps can handle on any given day. Triceps are tolerant of high-intensity training. Don't be afraid to pump up the volume.

> Triceps pressdowns: 5 sets, 10–15 reps (this applies to both
>   Phase 2 and Phase 3)

Next up is the lying-down triceps extension, also known as the lying French press (see chapter 3). The barbell comes down to your forehead, elbows bent, then you press the bar up overhead to arm's length. The movement allows you to pack on a lot of weight, but be careful—lifting too heavy on the first set could lead to a mishap, an elbow injury or (in a worst-case scenario) the bar could crash down on your head like a ton of bricks.

This should never happen. As long as you slowly increase the weight in the pyramid approach to lifting, your elbows stay healthy and your triceps respond to the stimulus. Never snap or jerk the elbow joints as you bend, and then extend, your elbows. Be especially careful at the top of the movement. I'm always conscious of the safety factor. In all my years of lifting I have never been injured. Accept responsibility for your actions in the gym; serious training is a serious business. Once you injure your elbows you can forget about a career in bodybuilding, not to mention golf, tennis, or even just playing ball with your kids.

> Lying-down triceps extensions: 4 sets, 8–10 reps (both Phase
>   2 and 3)

Now the two advanced workouts go their separate ways. Let's begin with Phase 2. I move from lying-down extensions to one-arm dumbbell extensions over the head (begin with one arm holding the dumbbell at arm's length, then lower in a semicircular motion behind your head until your forearm touches your biceps). Be sure to flex and squeeze the triceps for a complete contraction. Never snap or jerk the elbows; always go for a nice stretch as you bring the dumbbell back up to the top position.

> One-arm dumbbell extensions: 3–4 sets, 12–15 reps

One-arm dumbbell extension: Grasp a relatively-light dumbbell and bring it up and over your head with your arm extended. Following an arc, bring the dumbbell behind your head, flexing the triceps. Return to the starting position and repeat.

That's it for Phase 2; three exercises will suffice. Allow for three days of rest between workouts. Interestingly enough, Phase 3 is really quite similar to Phase 2—with two distinct exceptions: I might alternate lying-down triceps extensions (barbell) with standing extensions using a rope handle on a high cable/pulley apparatus. It's a nice change of pace; feel the different heads of the triceps fill with blood as you adjust the weight to suit your strength. I like using the rope; it's an effective method of overcoming your triceps training plateaus.

Standing cable triceps extensions: (with a rope handle attachment) 4 sets, 12–15 reps

Standing triceps extension with rope handle: **Attach a rope handle to an overhead pulley. Grasp the rope handle with both hands over your head, elbows bent, arms stretched as far back as possible. Now extend the triceps all the way outward until your elbows are straight. Slowly return to the starting position.**

Complete the Phase 3 workout with the reverse-grip (palm facing towards you, not away from you) one-arm cable extension. This angle of resistance isolates, and allows you to feel, the muscle expand as blood flows into the targeted area. Squeeze. Focus. Strive for perfection.

Reverse-grip one-arm cable extensions: 3 sets, 12–15 reps

That will do it for Phase 3. Again three days of rest between workouts is okay. Now, about seven to ten weeks before a show I'll add bench dips to this Phase 3 program. Just lower your body below bench level,

Reverse grip one-arm cable extension: **Grasp the handle of an overhead pulley with your palm facing you, elbow bent. Starting position: Your fist is at shoulder height, elbow is bent. Now press the handle down to straighten out your arm and extend your triceps, stretch, and bring the handle back up to the starting position. Repeat on the other arm.**

HANEY'S TRICEPS

PHASE 3 (HIGHEST INTENSITY)

EXERCISE	SETS	REPS
Triceps pressdown	5	10–15
Lying triceps extension (also known as a Lying French press)	4	8–10
Standing triceps extension with rope attachment	4–5	12–15
Reverse grip one-arm cable extension	3	12–15 (each arm)

PHASE 2 (INTERMEDIATE INTENSITY)

EXERCISE	SETS	REPS
Triceps pressdown	5	10–15
Lying triceps extension	4	8–10
One-arm dumbbell extension	3–4	12–15

PHASE 1 (MODERATE INTENSITY)

EXERCISE	SETS	REPS
Triceps pressdown	5	10–15
Lying triceps extension	4	8–10

(continued)

PRE-CONTEST (7–10 WEEKS BEFORE A SHOW)

EXERCISE	SETS	REPS
Triceps pressdown	5	10–15
Lying triceps extension or	4	8–10
Standing triceps extension with a rope handle	4	12–15
Reverse grip one-arm cable extension	3	12–15 (each arm)
Bench dip	3	10–15

feeling the contraction in your triceps, and keep your feet flat on the floor to ensure stability and safety.

I've seen some guys put weight plates in their laps (while doing the dips) to increase resistance. Who in their right mind would do such a thing? How can a weight plate in your lap help your triceps get bigger? If you want to up the resistance, ask your training partner to place his hands on your shoulders to apply a dab of added pressure.

Bench dips: 3 sets, 10–15 reps (pre-contest)

Phase 1 triceps training is just for maintaining what you already have built in Phase 2 and 3. Phase 1 (perfect for a beginner) is an "it's-better-than-nothing" type workout for Lee Haney. I'll rely on it after a long plane ride, exhausting work day or during Christmas vacation. The idea is to maintain, not overtrain. Never whip a tired horse!

Triceps pressdowns: 5 sets, 10–12 reps
Lying-down triceps extensions: 4 sets, 8–10 reps

All of these triceps programs are quick and easy. Allow for 35–45 seconds between exercises, 1 to 1½ minutes of rest between sets. My average workout—regardless of the specific bodypart—generally lasts no more than ninety minutes. Why spend hours hanging out in the gym? There's more to life than just lifting weights. Shoot for a high-intensity pump. Fill the targeted muscle with blood. Take your triceps to the limit. Again, stimulate; don't annihilate!

SECTION 5: HANEY'S BACK

One of my earliest childhood memories is my little sister screaming: "Move out of the way, big back!" She liked to call me "big back"—I had a wide back and a tiny waist, a nice symmetrical contrast that enhanced the natural V-shape of my torso.

My back is one of my best bodyparts. Never a problem getting it bigger. I rely on basic exercises that hit the latissimus dorsi (upper back muscles) from every angle, blending width, mass and definition into a simple program.

Phase 3

I don't switch off that much on back training. Everything stays pretty consistent. Start with wide-grip pulldowns. It's a rhythmic movement. Warm up the lats with a light set, then start packing on the weight to widen and sculpt your back.

You can do this exercise two ways: either pull the bar (at a pulldown station) down to your upper chest, or behind your head until it touches the back of your neck. I prefer the front pulldown variation. Here's why. After the 1984 Olympia I switched from back to front and immediately added size to my back. I could use more weight, get a better stretch, control the weight more effectively and enhance the isolation of the lower lumbar region.

If you want a bigger, thicker back and more overall definition, you must lift heavy. When doing pulldowns from behind, though, the higher poundages force you to start hunching forward, struggling to lift the weight. Go with front pulldowns. You're in more control; you can bring more muscle into play.

Wide-grip pull-up: **Assume a wide-grip (palms forward) on a pull-up bar. Come down for a full stretch, with your elbows and shoulders back. Then lift your body up—arching your back slightly—until your chin touches the bar. Be sure to stretch fully at the bottom of each rep.**

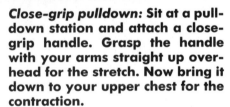

***Close-grip pulldown:* Sit at a pull-down station and attach a close-grip handle. Grasp the handle with your arms straight up overhead for the stretch. Now bring it down to your upper chest for the contraction.**

Now there's also the pressing issue of using a wide versus a close grip on the bar. The difference is obvious—a wide grip adds width; a close grip helps to stretch and elongate the lat muscles. Close-grip pulldowns are a nice finishing movement, comparable to concentration curls for biceps. Finally, you may want to toss in a few sets (as many as four) of wide-grip pull-ups. Some men can't lift their own bodyweight. If you can handle the resistance, though, pull-ups will add more width and shape to your lats.

Wide-grip pulldowns: 5 sets, 10–12 reps.
Close-grip pulldowns: 2–3 sets, 12–15 reps (optional)
Wide-grip pull-ups: 4 sets, maximum reps per set (optional)

T-bar row: **Stand on a platform at the T-bar station. Take a narrow grip on the handles and bend over until your torso is almost parallel to the floor. Slowly lower the bar for the stretch (your arms are fully extended) and then raise the T-bar up to chest height for the contraction.**

T-Bar Rows

An explosive, mass-building exercise. The T-bar packs on the meat! And you need to beef-up the lats if size and thickness are what you're after. Stay away from the new style of T-bar with a chest pad and an incline platform for your feet. That position places a lot of stress on the erector spinae muscles of the lower back. And you can end up looking like a hunchback; the incline platform prods you into a humpbacked posture.

I tried this new-wave T-bar after pulling a hamstring when I was training in Texas with Evander Holyfield. I could rest on my tummy and do this pretty little exercise. What a waste of time! No new muscle growth. No new cuts. A big zero.

The proper version of the T-bar relies on a small, flat platform. Your back is arched. Your shoulders and head are right up over the plates, knees slightly bent. Grasp the handles and lift the weight up towards your chest; feel the contraction, then lower and go for the stretch.

T-bar rows: 4 sets, 6–8 reps

Seated cable rows

A rhythmic movement, and an effective means of isolating the lat muscles. Take it nice and slow. Lean forward—elongating your muscles—for the stretch. Then pull the handles to your upper abdomen for a complete contraction. Always arch your back in the positive, muscle contraction, phase of the exercise.

Don't let your muscles relax as you extend the arms forward for a stretch. This elongation, or negative, mode of training demands maintaining constant tension. Stay in control. Never allow your mind to wander.

Seated cable rows: 4 sets, 12–15 reps

Barbell bent-over rows

The bread and butter of back training. An explosive movement with an attitude. From a bent-over position, bring the bar up from just-above-floor level until it touches your lower abdomen (See chapter 3 for photographs of this exercise). Feel the contraction. Visualize as you

Seated cable row: **Place a bench in front of a low pulley; sit on the bench, grasp the handles with a close grip and place your feet against the foot pad (or platform) for support, knees slightly bent. Extend your arms and bend forward, feeling the stretch in your lats. Now pull the handle back to your upper abs—your back should arch and your chest should stick out. Return to the stretched position and repeat for the desired number of reps.**

train. Link the mind and muscle together. No other exercise will build as much mass, thickness, and quality. I prefer the bar to dumbbells. You can kill two birds with one stone—hit both sides of the lats at once—and get through your workout quickly and efficiently.

Barbell bent-over rows: 4 sets, 6–8 reps

The Phase 3 program requires at least three days of rest between workouts. It's my main back training plan, the one I go with in the off-season to build the muscle mass needed to win Mr. Olympia titles.

Phase 2 & Phase 1

Phase 2 is essentially the same as Phase 3, with one exception: I drop the T-bar rows and just do the other three exercises. Sets and reps remain the same as in Phase 3. Phase 1 is only two exercises—wide-grip pulldowns (rhythmic) and barbell bent-over rows (explosive). It's a great

HANEY'S BACK

PHASE 3

EXERCISE	SETS	REPS
Wide-grip pulldown	5	10–12
Wide-grip pull-up*	4	Max
T-bar row	4	6–8
Seated cable row	4	12–15
Barbell bent-over row	4	6–8
Close-grip pulldown*	2–3	10–12

*optional

PHASE 2

EXERCISE	SETS	REPS
Wide-grip pulldown	5	10–12
Barbell bent-over row	4	6–8
Seated cable row	4	12–15

PHASE 1

EXERCISE	SETS	REPS
Wide-grip pulldown	5	10–12
Barbell bent-over row	4	6–8

(continued)

PRE-CONTEST (7–10 WEEKS BEFORE A SHOW)

EXERCISE	SETS	REPS
Wide-grip pulldown	5	10–12
One-arm dumbbell row*	4	6–8
Barbell bent-over row*	4	6–8
Seated cable row	4	12–15
T-bar row#	4	6–8

*alternate these two exercises,
   one per workout.
#perform this movement every
   third workout.

beginner's workout, one I use after traveling for twenty hours. Doing only two exercises means I can slip in a quick pump without any fuss or bother.

Pre-Contest

Again, I don't make any major changes. I flip-flop barbell rows with one-arm dumbbell rows in the last seven weeks before a show. The dumbbells force me to kick back on the weight a little, but it's better for isolation. Four weeks before the contest I'll only do the one-arm dumbbell rows—it's very unlikely you'll pack on mass this late in the game. T-bars become an occasional thing, not a staple, in the last seven weeks of training. Remember that T-bars build width. How much width can you expect to build in the last few weeks before a contest? In the final analysis, consistent application of the Phase 3 workout is the only way to build a back like Lee Haney's—the original "big back" of his family.

One-arm dumbbell row: **Place the knee and hand of the arm not holding the dumbbell on a flat bench for support. Grasp a medium-weight dumbbell and allow it to rest just above floor level—your arm is fully extended. Then bring the dumbbell upward until it reaches the outer portion of the pec. Lower for the stretch and repeat.**

SECTION 6: HANEY'S CHEST

My chest program has always been on the money. Never a problem. Blast those pectoral muscles with the mass-building (explosive) exercises, then fire away with lighter weight on the quality (rhythmic) movements. Never accept anything but the best; if you do the work, I guarantee you'll enjoy the results.

Phase 3

A serious program—not too crazy, but very intense. Warm up with a light weight on the barbell bench press. Visualize a massive, powerful chest. Now set your sights on growth and glory. Let's get busy: Start with four sets of heavy barbell bench presses (6–8 reps); there's no substitute for this basic explosive movement. Done properly, it will always enlarge the size of your chest in a symmetrical, precise manner (See chapter 3 for photographs of the exercise). Then I follow up with three sets of heavy dumbbell presses (10–12 reps), varying the weight from 90–130 pounds depending on how I feel that day.

Dumbbell bench press: **Lie on a flat bench with a heavy dumbbell in each hand. Hold the dumbbells at arm's length, palms facing forward. Lower the dumbbells straight down to the sides of your chest. Push back up to the starting position and repeat.**

You must listen to your body each time you walk into the gym. Is it telling you to go easy? Fine. Back off on the weight and do a few more reps, or just pyramid the weight gradually until you're ready for the high end of your maximum strength lifts. I may pyramid from 90 to 130 pounds on the dumbbell bench press. I may stick with the 90–100 pounders. Trust your instincts. If you grab those dumbbells and they feel like a ton, then scale back down to a lighter weight.

After the two basic bench presses—explosive movements that build the overall size of your pecs—I work up to the incline exercises. Barbell incline presses (3 sets, 6–8 reps) and dumbbell incline presses (2–3 sets, 10–12 reps) add thickness to the upper pecs. You're building meat, packing on beef, via explosive high-intensity training.

Intensity flows from flip-flopping barbell and dumbbell variations on the same theme. With the standard barbell press, for instance, all

Dumbbell incline bench press: Again, lie back on an incline bench set at a 30 degree angle. Hold the dumbbells at arm's length above you, bring them down to your upper chest, and shoot them back up to a straight-out position.

Dumbbell flye: **I like to do this at various bench positions to hit the pectoral muscles from a variety of angles. Holding the dumbbells overhead and facing each other, gradually lower and widen the arc until the bottom portion of the dumbbells is aligned with your front deltoids. Then, without releasing the tension in your chest muscles, drive the dumbbells upward; you're retracing the path of the descent until you reach the starting position.**

emphasis is on controlling as heavy a weight as possible for 6–8 reps. When you switch to dumbbells, though, you take the reps a tad higher, the weight a lot lower, and prioritize pumping blood into the muscle. Same agenda for the incline barbell and dumbbell presses: explosive thrusts on the bar, designed to build mass and power; explosive lifts of the dumbbells, but with that intuitive awareness that you're forcing more blood into the upper pecs.

Once I finish the incline dumbbell presses, I move to dumbbell flyes (3–4 sets, 12–15 reps), a rhythmic exercise that isolates the pecs. Presses build size; flyes add quality to the shape of the muscle. The flye movement—lowering the dumbbells out to each side of the chest in a semicircular motion—is so simple and natural; feel the deep contraction at the bottom of the movement and then retrace your path back up to the starting position (dumbbells at arm's length above you, palms facing each other).

Cable crossover: **Standing midway between the crossover pulleys, grasp one handle in each hand. Keep a slight bend in your arms and bend forward at the waist. Then slowly pull the cable inward until your hands are almost touching in front of your waist. Slowly return to the starting position and repeat.**

On deck is the infamous cable crossover (3 sets, 15–20 reps): Bring each cable handle across your chest, squeeze, and release; it's the perfect stretch-and-contract motion for added definition. Then finish the workout with parallel bar dips—lower your body as far as possible by bending the arms, elbows close in to your sides, then press back up to arm's length—to hit your lower chest. The dip session (3 sets, 15 reps) is tiring, especially after all those other exercises. You'll be begging for mercy. But don't worry—Phase 3 demands three to four days of recovery time for your pecs. You can use that time to contemplate how much better you look for all your sweat and effort.

HANEY'S CHEST

PHASE 1

EXERCISE	SETS	REPS
Barbell bench press	4–5	6–8
Incline barbell bench press	4–5	6–8
Dumbbell flye	3–4	12–15

PHASE 2

EXERCISE	SETS	REPS
Barbell bench press	5	6–8
Incline barbell bench press	4–5	6–8
Dumbbell flye	3–4	12–15
Cable crossover	3–4	15–20
Dip*	3	15

*every other workout

PHASE 3

EXERCISE	SETS	REPS
Barbell bench press	4–5	6–8
Dumbbell bench press	3–4	10–12
Barbell incline bench press	3	6–8
Dumbbell incline bench press	2–3	10–12
Dumbbell flye	3–4	12–15
Cable crossover	3	15–20
Dip	3	15

Pre-Contest (7–10 weeks before a show)
Alternate Phase Two and Phase Three.

Phase 2

Another workout blending mass and quality. Begin with barbell bench presses (5 sets, 6–8 reps) and incline barbell bench presses (4–5 sets, 6–8 reps) for the beef, then do your dumbbell flyes (3–4 sets, 12–15 reps), cable crossovers (3–4 sets, 20 reps) and dips (3 sets, 15 reps, every other workout) for quality and proportionality. Take three days off between workouts.

Phase 1

Where's the beef? You'll find it right here at Lee's mass-building seminar: barbell bench presses, incline barbell bench presses and flyes (same sets and reps as in Phase 2). This is a fast and intense workout, a fantastic pump and growth spurt for the pecs. And you only need three days of rest between workouts.

Dip: **Hold your body at arm's length above a parallel bar. Now lower yourself as far as possible—press back up to the starting position and flex your lower pecs at the top. The more you lean forward, the more you'll work your chest.**

Pre-Contest

I switch back and forth between Phase 2 and Phase 3. Different levels of intensity keep the muscles guessing what's coming next. "What the heck is Haney doing?" Forget it. I'm not going to let on for a minute. Stimulation is a guessing game; surprise your pecs with varying workouts at varying levels of resistance. Allow for the necessary recovery time. I've never been injured and I've been at this training business for twenty years. No tears. No pulls. No joint or ligament damage. I know what I'm doing; follow my lead and you can share the same injury-free success.

SECTION 7: HANEY'S SHOULDERS

Along with my chest, this is one area that's been a piece of cake. Stimulating the deltoids is easy as breaking a sweat on a humid day in Atlanta. Hit the muscle from every angle and you cannot go wrong.

The Off-Season Strategy

I cycle my workouts, switching back and forth between two basic programs. About eight to ten weeks before a show, I pump up the volume and go crazy. Let's move in sequence from my easiest shoulder training plan to the toughest, the pre-contest shock-effect special.

Phase 1

Start with front military press with a barbell, not dumbbells, for five sets. Go light on the first set. Let your front delts ease into a pattern of resistance. Lift the bar from shoulder height to arm's length, feel the contraction in your front delts, and lower the bar. This is an explosive movement. You can lift a lot of weight. Bear in mind, though, that you don't want to kill the shoulders in the first set of your workout. Pyramid the poundages. Focus on quality lifts. Feel free to stay in the 8–10 rep range for the first three sets; shoulders need more warm-up time than most other bodyparts. Shoot for 6–8 reps for at least the last two sets.

I like to alternate front barbell presses with behind-the-neck presses—place the bar on your upper back, then press it overhead to arm's length and return to the initial phase. I often start the workout,

Behind-the-neck military press (barbell): **Sit on a bench positioned beneath a rack. Place the bar on your upper back, hands 4 to 7 inches beyond shoulder width. Press the bar up to arm's length, then lower to the starting position.**

though, with a few warm-up sets of front presses. If you work behind-the-neck for starters, well, it's not what I would call comfortable. How many heavy objects do you put behind your neck and then lift over your head? Natural? Not exactly. But behind-the-neck presses do stimulate muscle growth. Done properly, after the shoulders are ready for action, they are safe and effective. You can't go without them, at least every other workout.

> Front military presses: 5 sets, 6–8 reps
> Behind-the-neck military presses: 5 sets, 6–8 reps

Move from an explosive movement to a rhythmic movement, the classic lateral raise (see chapter 3 for photographs of the exercise). I see some guys lifting heavy dumbbells, straining and gagging as they try to bring the weights up to shoulder height. Not so bright. Okay, it's down-right dumb. How many times a day do you pick anything up with both of your arms out to your sides? And with a heavy weight? You're looking for trouble. I never use a lot of weight with lateral raises. Twenty-five to 35 pounders do the trick, stimulate growth in the medial (side) deltoid like nothing else in this world.

> Lateral raises: 4 sets, 10–12 reps

I finish Phase 1 with heavy upright rows from behind. Bring the barbell up over your butt to mid-back level, squeezing the trapezius and rear delts. Just bend your elbows and raise the bar. Powerful stuff. And, yes, it is an unusual exercise. A friend of mine took photos of my traps before and after I started doing this movement in 1982. The pictures told the whole story: My traps had grown like crazy in a short time.

> Reverse upright rows: 3 sets, 8–10 reps

Allow for three days of recovery after the Phase 1 workout.

Phase 2

Do a warm-up set of front barbell presses (8–10 reps). Put the bar on your upper back and blast out four sets of behind-the-neck presses (6–8 reps). Then switch to dumbbell front presses (4 sets, 6–8 reps) for a slightly different feeling in your front delts. Same movement as front barbell presses, but the dumbbells give you that extra touch of muscle

Reverse upright row: **Grasp a heavy barbell with a palms-up grip. Starting position: The bar is behind your hamstrings. Focusing on your rear deltoids and trapezius, bend at the elbows (shrugging your shoulders slightly) and raise the bar above butt level. Squeeze, lower and repeat for the desired number of reps.**

Front military press (dumbbell): Sit comfortably at the end of a flat bench with a dumbbell in each hand. Raise the dumbbells to shoulder height with a palms-down grip on the weights. Keep your elbows out, thumbs facing in. Press the dumbbells to arm's length overhead, then return to the starting position.

awareness; always lift each weight up evenly on both sides of your body. Emphasize perfect symmetry, from front to back, side to side.

Now switch to the rhythmic movements: lateral raises (same sets and reps as Phase 1) and bent-over (or reverse) laterals, where you raise two dumbbells as you would with a lateral raise, but perform the movement by bending over slightly at the waist so that your torso is parallel to the ground. Pull the dumbbells upward in a hugging motion—elbows slightly bent at the top. Pause with the dumbbells held at about head

HANEY'S SHOULDERS

PHASE 2

EXERCISE	SETS	REPS
Behind-the-neck military press#	5*	6–8
Front military press (with dumbbells)	4	6–8
Lateral raise	4	10–12
Bent-over lateral raise	4	10–12
Upright row or	3–4	12–15
Reverse upright row	3	8–10

*first set is a warm-up
#do one set of front shoulder
presses as a warm-up

PHASE 1

EXERCISE	SETS	REPS
Front military press#	5*	6–8
Behind-the-neck military press#	5*	6–8
Lateral raise	4	10–12
Reverse upright row	3	8–10

*first set is a warm-up
#alternate workouts

(continued)

PHASE 3/PRE-CONTEST
(8–10 WEEKS BEFORE A SHOW)

EXERCISE	SETS	REPS
Front military press	3–4	10–12
Behind-the-neck military press	3–4	10–12
Lateral raise	3	12–15
Cable lateral raise (one arm at a time)	3	12–15
Bent-over lateral raise	3	12–15
Bent-over cable lateral raise	3	12–15
Reverse upright row	4	8–10

level, and make sure that the descent is slow and controlled. The bent-over position works rear deltoid, an often overlooked part of the deltoid complex. Do 4 sets, 10–12 reps.

Finish with either reverse upright rows (same sets and reps as Phase 1) or regular upright rows: bringing the bar from arm's length to your chin or upper chest by bending at the elbows. Upright rows demand lighter weights (than the reverse variation) so increase reps to 12–15 for 3 or 4 sets.

Allow for three days of recovery after the Phase 2 workout.

Bent-over lateral raise: Bend at the waist until your back is almost parallel to the floor. Hold the dumbbells in front of you at shin height, palms facing inward. Pull the dumbbells upward in a hugging motion—elbows slightly bent at the top. Lower and repeat.

Upright row: Assume a close, palms-down grip on the barbell at thigh level. Bend at the elbows and pull the bar up to your upper chest (or chin). Pause, then lower the bar to the starting position.

Phase 3

Whew, get ready for my pre-contest formula for unearthing those freaky cuts and striations. I'm serious. Pump up the volume with higher reps (10–12) and lighter weight for the explosive movements (front and behind-the-neck barbell presses). Lighter weight, yes; however, it's still a "hard" 10–12 reps. Don't move the weight in slow motion—it's just a heave; thrust forward with control, good form and with a weight you can handle.

I prefer the bar to dumbbells. I enjoy the way it pumps up my shoulders. No thinking about balancing each weight. I just do it. Dumbbells slow down the process. And I want to get through this as quick as I can and move on to the next exercise.

The next exercise in this workout is the lateral raise; first with a dumbbell, then with a cable. The cable enables you to isolate the medial

Lateral raise (cable): **Stand between two floor-level pulleys. Grasp a handle in each hand and cross one handle over the other. Now bring each handle out—mimicking the motion you'd use with a dumbbell on a standard lateral raise—to full extension, squeeze your side delts, then return to the starting position.**

delt more than a dumbbell does. That's the beauty of cable exercise. It provides continuous tension, forcing more and more blood into the targeted area. Pump as much blood into the muscle as possible to bring about muscle fusion—the muscle cell splits, adding size and giving you that striated appearance on stage. The rest of the program targets rear delts and trapezius; again, working the shoulder at every angle of resistance is the best plan of action if you're serious about bodybuilding.

Bent-over lateral raise (cable): **Stand in-between two low cable pulleys; stand far enough away to create tension on the cable. Bend until your back is parallel to the floor, cross one handle over another at shin height, and bring each handle outward until you exhaust the range of motion in your medial (side) delts. Let the handles slowly return to the starting position and repeat.**

Lateral raises: 3 sets, 12–15 reps
Cable laterals: 3 sets, 12–15 reps (one arm at a time)
Bent-over laterals: 3 sets, 12–15 reps
Bent-over cable laterals: 3 sets, 12–15 reps
Reverse upright rows: 4 sets, 10–12 reps

Take three or four days off after this Phase 3 killer. In fact, always allow for three or four recovery days after a shoulder workout; the delts get plenty of work (whether they like it or not) when you train chest. Adequate recovery time is an important element in the muscle-growth equation.

SECTION 8: HANEY'S ABDOMINALS
(Workouts #1 and 2)

Keep constant tabs on your abs. Never let down your guard. If you can see your rectus abdominis (the main ab muscle running from your ribcage to your pelvis), then you're within striking distance of success.

Training abdominals is a serious matter. I need to know that I'm in control of my physique. If I don't see my abs I get very, very scared— *Okay, Lee, you are starting to lose control of your body. It's time to get a grip.*

Look, this is what I do for a living. I'm not out for a spring walk in the park. If you can't flex it, don't carry it! Stay on top of your abdominal development. Train every other day. Work up to five days a week in the Pre-Contest Phase. Monitor your diet carefully; never allow more than 10 or 15 percent of your daily calories to come from fat-based sources.

There's no need, though, to starve yourself or do eight million abdominal exercises. Adhere to a sensible diet (see my chapter on nutrition) and do three or four effective movements at least every other day. Why overtrain? Stay on track; get ripped with my time-tested approach.

Workout #1: Incline sit-ups

Begin with this very basic exercise. Completely effective. Lie back on an incline board, secure your feet under the pads, curl up about half way, squeezing your ribcage and pelvis together and flexing your abs. Move slowly. Rely on your abdominal strength—not momentum—to complete each rep. Don't flop up and down like a fish out of water. Focus on the squeeze; isolate the muscle; build a sharp set of abs without screwing up your back or annihilating the muscle.

Incline sit-up, with twist: **Same position as the incline sit-up (see chapter 3 photograph). In this variation, though, you bring your right elbow toward your left knee—and vice versa—to work intercostals and serratus. Exhale on the contraction.**

Incline sit-ups: 4 sets, 15–20 reps

VARIATION: I'll come up and twist to one side or the other to develop the intercostals and serratus. I do at least ten reps on both right and left sides of the body per workout.

Vertical leg raises

The key here is to crunch your abs together, not just swing at the hips. Grasp the handles of a vertical leg raise station and rest your elbows on the pads. Hang straight up and down and lift your legs—don't swing them too high via momentum. Crunch at the top as you rock the knees up and bring the body forward. Rolling upward—crunching your abs—brings both lower and upper abdominals into play.

Vertical leg raises: 3 sets, 15–20 reps

Vertical leg raise: **Grasp the handles of a vertical leg raise station and rest your elbows on the pads. Hang straight up and down, then lift your knees up as you crunch your pelvis towards your ribcage. Pause, then lower your legs and repeat.**

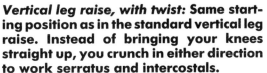

Vertical leg raise, with twist: **Same starting position as in the standard vertical leg raise. Instead of bringing your knees straight up, you crunch in either direction to work serratus and intercostals.**

VARIATION: Perform the vertical leg raise with a twist to stimulate the serratus and intercostals. Never ignore your serratus and intercostals, those abdominal muscles on the side of your torso. Heck, you can't win an Olympia without impressive serratus definition. Just glance back at Samir in '83 for ample proof of what a ripped serratus can do for your posing.

Vertical leg raises with a twist: 2 sets, 10 reps per side

HANEY'S ABDOMINALS

OFF-SEASON WORKOUT #1

EXERCISE	SETS	REPS
Incline sit-up	4	15–20
Vertical leg raise	3	15–20
Vertical leg raise with a twist	2	10 on each side
Seated leg raise	3	10–15

OFF-SEASON WORKOUT #2

EXERCISE	SETS	REPS
Incline sit-up	4	15–20
Vertical leg raise	3	15–20
Vertical leg raise with a twist	2	10 on each side
Cable crunch	4	15–20

PRE-CONTEST

Repeat Workout #2 but add

Standing side twist:	3	20

Seated leg raises

This exercise had many names—seated leg raise, jackknife sit-up—but the form remains the same: Sit at the edge of a bench with your legs extended, then bend your knees and pull your upper thighs in toward your chest. Exhale on the contraction (this is true of all ab exercises) and inhale on the stretch.

Seated leg raises: 3 sets, 10–15 reps
Perform Abdominal Workout #1 every other day.

Workout #2

Same sets and reps for incline sit-ups, vertical leg raises, and the variations to hit your serratus. Replace the seated leg raise with a standing cable crunch: Attach a rope handle to a pulley and lean forward to grasp a handle in either hand—your arms are outstretched in front of

Cable crunch: **I prefer to do this exercise from a standing position; this gives me a more complete "pull" than the kneeling position. Attach a rope handle to a pulley and lean forward to grasp a handle in each hand—your arms are outstretched in front of you. Now bend over and pull the handle down, crunching your ribcage and pelvis together. Pause at the bottom, then return to the top for the stretch.**

Side twists with a stick: **Stand with a broomhandlelike stick resting on your shoulders. Twist your torso completely from side to side—your hands control the stick to ensure proper balance. Always flex your abs as you twist; keep the motion controlled and continuous throughout the entire set.**

you. Now bend over and pull the handle down, crunching your ribcage and pelvis together. Pause at the bottom, then return to the top for the stretch.

Perform Abdominal Workout #2 every other day.

Pre-Contest

I maintain my ab workout #2, but increase frequency (five times a week) and add the twist (with a stick, not a barbell or dumbbells). Hold a stick behind your back and twist your torso first to the right, then to the left. Twist only at the waist. Keep your back straight, head up. Inhale to the center; exhale as you twist to either side.

Twists limber up the back and condition the serratus to squeezing and flexing. When you're up on stage in the lineup you want those bad boys to look as sharp as possible. Twists enhance your muscle control; they do not build muscle or add definition per se. It's more of a posing thing, as you can taper your waist while isolating and squeezing the targeted muscles.

Twists: 3 sets, 20 reps

That's it for my ab routine. I'll always do three movements per workout. If I do four exercises, I split it up this way: Two exercises in the morning, two exercises in the evening. Remember that it's impossible to burn fat through abdominal work. The only way to shed excess blubber is through a low-fat diet and aerobic exercise.

SECTION 9: HANEY'S AEROBICS

Aerobic exercise is a necessity for all bodybuilders. You must burn calories to stay sleek and defined. There's a fine line, though, between burning calories and depleting your stores of glycogen—a starchlike fuel in the muscle that's converted into simple sugar. High-intensity aerobics (beyond 65 percent of your maximum heart rate or MHR) cuts into your glycogen reserves, overtaxing the muscle and promoting a disappearing act. All that hard-earned muscle mass fades into nothing. Where did it go? Out the door with the unwanted fat!

I stick with low-impact aerobics. Consistent. On target for a body-builder's goals. Never beyond 65 percent of my MHR. Most modern cardiovascular equipment allows you to monitor your heart rate on the display console.

Daily Aerobics

Typically, I'll squeeze in my aerobic exercise after my morning lifting. Fifteen minutes on the stationary bike, then fifteen minutes on the treadmill. I'm flexible. Some days I'll pack it in after fifteen minutes on the bike. If I'm taking care of business in downtown Atlanta, or training

Stationary biking.

HANEY'S AEROBICS

45–60 minutes, 4–5 times a week at moderate intensity.

After the morning workout: 15 minutes on the stationary bike; 15 minutes of treadmill or 15–20 minutes of speedwalking.

After the evening workout: 15 minutes on the stationary bike; 15 minutes on the treadmill.

Workout at roughly 65 percent of your maximum heart rate (MHR). Your MHR is calculated by subtracting your age from 220. If you're 30, your MHR is 190 beats per minute.

Haney on the move, burning calories and working those calves by speedwalking.

at the Animal Kingdom, I may speedwalk for fifteen minutes up and down a few city blocks.

After my evening weight workout, if I'm not too tired, it's back on the bike and/or treadmill for fifteen to twenty minutes. My goal is forty-five to sixty minutes of aerobics a day. Forget about doing the bike or treadmill after a leg session. I'm lucky if I can climb a set of stairs! Squats and heavy leg presses put the whammy on any cardiovascular training.

SECTION 10: HANEY'S ADVANCED BODYBUILDING SCHEDULE

Stick with an on three, off one format—three days of training, then kick back from the weights. Use your off day to prioritize aerobic exercise.

I believe in the Push Pull Principle of splitting bodyparts: combine a pushing muscle group (chest) with a pulling muscle group (back). Never do two pulling exercises in the same workout. A little background: In the old days (pre-1983 Olympia) I'd pair biceps with back. This was my strategy for the Mr. Universe, the Nationals, and the Atlantic USA. After preparing for those three shows I was hurting; my shoulders were so raw I could barely pick up a 45-pound bar. My poor tendons and joints were inflamed. The pain was killing me! No more pairing chest and shoulders, two pushing muscle groups. No more of this back and biceps nonsense! The guys in California set me straight—the Push Pull Principle protects your shoulders, prevents injury, and keeps your muscles fresh and ready for growth.

Day #1

MORNING WORKOUT: Biceps (pull), Chest (push), stationary bike, treadmill or speedwalking, 15–30 minutes.

EVENING: Triceps (push), calves, abdominals, 15–30 minutes on the stationary bike.

Day #2

Frontal thigh (push) in the morning; hamstrings (pull) in the evening. No bike; there's a lot of suffering going on!

Day #3

Back (pull), abdominals and aerobics in the morning. Shoulders (push), calves and aerobics in the evening.

Day #4

(No lifting.) I wake up early and hit the bike for thirty minutes, or I do a combination of jogging and speedwalking for thirty to forty-five minutes. I don't use this day to sit around and watch the Georgia clay crack—I'm always doing something to stay in shape.

That's not to say, though, that working out should overwhelm your entire life. Budget time for simple pleasures. Get too obsessed in the off-season and you'll be dead by the time your contest rolls around.

5

THE MR. OLYMPIA DIET

All the cards were on the table in 1991—it was a critical year in my life. I didn't want to go down in history as the guy who won seven Mr. Olympia titles and blew it the last time around. I didn't want to second guess myself: *If only I hadn't entered that eighth show—I could have been unquestionably the best*. I had that kind of pressure on me.

Coping with pressure is part of the Mr. Olympia job description. When you're at the top of the heap, well, everyone is gunning for your title. I had a lot of important decisions to make. What will I eat to ensure that my physique looks sharp? What supplements will I take? Choices.

I had to sort through all the different diet and nutritional plans available to a bodybuilder. But, hey, it's not as if I was starting from scratch—I had eight years of trial and error to fall back on. The preparation for 1991 actually seemed easy, like I wasn't even making sacrifices. After careful reflection and analysis, I knew exactly what path to follow.

Let's take a quick look back at recent history. I competed in Rimini (the sixth Olympia title) at 257 pounds, a humungozoid—big and impressive. In 1990 (in Chicago), I was leaner but still not quite perfect.

The objective for 1991 was to come in sharp and ripped, with the size needed to destroy the competition.

THE 1991 MR. OLYMPIA PROGRAM

Remember my motto: "If you can't flex it, don't carry it." Stay lean and in-shape all the time. Never allow fat to cover your abdominal muscles—even in the off-season. I want to see my abs year-round. And yet I also want to build considerable muscle mass.

No problem. The harder I train, the more calories I put into my body. In the off-season, for instance, my caloric intake is 3,400 to 4,000 calories. As I lead up to a contest I'll jump up to 5,000 calories per day. The secret is to pull those calories from quality, low-fat nutrients while staying on a consistent aerobic program (see chapter 3).

Things change. In my earliest years of training I'd emphasize the heavier complex carbohydrates—pasta, potatoes, yams, and grains. A baked potato at every meal will take its toll on your digestive system. You walk around with a stuffy feeling. Then it's time to train and you're feeling really bloated. Man, that's one of the most uncomfortable sensations in the world—lifting heavy weights knowing full well that you still haven't digested your last meal. It reached the point where I had to say to myself: *Lee, you've got to cut back on some of those heavy carbs.*

By combining lighter carbohydrates—oatmeal and whole-wheat bread—with easy-to-digest vegetables (spinach, for instance) I was on my way to success. Simple carbs, specifically fresh fruit, also played an important role in my diet. Strawberries, pineapple packed in its own juice, pears, apples, and Georgia peaches arrived on my training table to enhance digestion and support high-intensity performance. Quick energy—that's the beauty of simple carbs.

Live and learn. I'm getting older. My metabolism and my body's ability to burn calories is slowing down a bit. But I'm making the necessary adjustments, keeping up-to-date with the changing demands of my metabolism—and the latest research in bodybuilding food science—to stay ahead of the aging process.

That research certainly doesn't indicate that bodybuilders or athletes should deep-six all of the heavier complex carbs. I eat my share of rice, breads, pasta, potatoes, and oatmeal. I'm just not fanatic about cramming as much food as possible into every sitting. Lighter, more frequent meals are the ticket to substantive gains in size and lean muscle mass.

Here's my pre-Olympia diet plan. Six meals a day. A nice balance of protein (25 percent of total calories), carbohydrates (65 percent) and fats (10 percent). Avoid dairy products and red meat. Never eat fried foods, as they're high in cholesterol and saturated fat.

Begin with Meal #1:

Omelette—2 whole eggs and 6–7 egg whites
Oatmeal—with strawberries and maple syrup or honey
5 ozs. pineapple (packed in its own juice)
Water
Black coffee

NOTE: The egg whites, of course, are an excellent source of nonfat protein; all the fat in eggs comes from the yolks. I may toss in a little skim milk mozzarella, spinach, onions, and other vegetables. But I eliminate the cheese four months before a contest. Drink water with every meal and during your training. Purge your system of toxins and replenish your body's natural fluids to ward off dehydration and exhaustion.

Next, comes your Morning Workout.

Then, follow with Meal #2:

2 broiled chicken breasts
1 baked potato
Sauteed spinach
5 ozs. pineapple
2 slices of whole-wheat toast
Water

NOTES: Pull the skin (the fat source) off of the chicken. Cook the spinach without butter. Put jam or preserves—instead of butter or other fat-based spreads—on your toast.

Next, take a ninety-minute nap.

Then, follow with Meal #3:

Tuna (packed in spring water)
Rice
Pineapple
Water

NOTES: Any fruit will suffice. I love pineapple—it's so easy to digest. Avoid tuna packed in oil. Stay away from mayonnaise.

After several hours follow with Meal #4.

Whole-wheat pancakes with syrup (with banana)
Black coffee
Water

NOTES: This is just a light snack. Waffles or French toast are fine; any complex-carb that's not too filling will do the trick. I generally share this meal with my son, Josh, after I pick him up from school in the afternoon. We horse around a little, play football or baseball in the yard. By the end of the "Josh Hour" I'm ready to get back into the gym.
   This is the Evening Workout.
   Followed by Meal #5:

Chicken or fish
Spinach or another steamed vegetable
Rice or noodles
5 ozs. pineapple
2 pieces of whole-wheat toast
Water

NOTES: Vary your choices. Enjoy a variety of fish dishes. Don't allow your daily diet to become dull and predictable.
   Meal #6, the final meal of the day, should be light:

Fruit Salad or
Bowl of oatmeal with strawberries

NOTES: Nice and easy. Don't go to bed with a full stomach. The fruit digests quickly and efficiently.

DAILY SUPPLEMENTATION

I supplement my diet with a high potency vitamin/mineral tablet. The added vitamins and minerals assure rapid assimilation of nutrients, while also protecting muscles, joints, and ligaments against an injury during hard training. As I get closer to a competition, I'll take an extra B-complex and C-complex with bioflavinoids to improve recuperation between workouts. C-complex helps to repair connective tissue in skin, ligaments, and bones.
   I'm a firm believer in herbal supplements. They improve recovery

and increase energy output. Nature's Herbs makes three herbal supplements well worth considering:

Sports Vitamins With Herbs

Take this with the morning meal. It's a combination of vitamins (including L-Carnitine), minerals (patented Chromium Picolinate), and herbs (including Milk Thistle extract).

ADVANTAGE: The herbs produce an energizing effect, balancing metabolism and strengthening the body's natural defenses. Taken regularly, the herbs will minimize muscle soreness from high-intensity training.

Sports Ginseng

Take this five minutes before each workout. Sports Ginseng contains a full 100 mgs. each of Korean and Siberian Ginsengs.

ADVANTAGE: It helps build physical endurance and improve performance. A nice alternative to a double espresso before a workout.

Sports Adaptogen (Russian Formula)

Take this mix (it contains Ginseng and Schizandra) after each workout.

ADVANTAGE: It will help your body resist stress, delay muscle fatigue and improve recovery.

Those are the basic supplements in the daily plan. Consider three other supplement options for specific applications to training: GH Fuel (includes natural growth hormone releasers Arginine and Ornithine); TwinLab Chromic Fuel (with chromium picolinate for enhanced workout intensity); and TwinLab Mass Fuel (to add low-fat calories to your diet when there's not enough time to eat six meals, or when you're looking to add muscle mass without unwanted fat).

All of these products are safe, natural and scientifically tested for effectiveness.

A Word About Steroids

Anabolic steroids are illegal and harmful. Follow my diet and supplement plan and you'll never need to take steroids to cheat your way to success. Unconvinced? Here are just a few of the possible adverse side effects of anabolic steroids:

1. Cardiovascular diseases (such as decreased HDL-cholesterol, increased LDL-cholesterol, increased total cholesterol, increased blood triglycerides, and hypertension)
2. Liver diseases (such as hepatitis, benign and malignant liver tumors and liver function abnormalities)
3. Reproductive diseases (such as prostate cancer, testicular atrophy, and infertility)
4. Impaired humoral immune responses (antibody production)
5. Acne
6. Behavioral changes/Psychiatric disorders

PERSONALIZING YOUR CALORIC INTAKE

Not everyone is built like yours truly. Gear your total daily caloric consumption to your particular body type and, of course, your level of physical activity. It's as easy as matching up your physique with one of the three basic body types:

The Mesomorph Profile

A fast metabolism. Naturally muscular with broad shoulders and a slim waist. Puts on muscle-mass easily. Nutritional focus is on complex carbs—my diet is a good case study.

EXAMPLES: Lee Haney and Arnold.

The Ectomorph Profile

A fast metabolism. Burns calories with ease. It's a double-edged sword: An ectomorph doesn't have to worry about getting fat, but has great difficulty adding any quality mass. Nutritional focus is on 15—instead of 10—percent of daily calories coming from fat-based sources, and getting enough quality calories from protein and complex carbs.

EXAMPLES: Frank Zane (three-time Mr. Olympia) and Evander Holyfield.

The Endomorph Profile

A slow metabolism. Holds excess body fat. Needs to rely on a low-fat diet. Typical protein sources: chicken (no skin), turkey, fish, and eggs (no yolks). The vast majority of an endomorph's calories should come from simple carbohydrates and green, leafy vegetables. Limit complex carb consumption to the early part of the day. Increase aerobic activity to burn additional fat.

EXAMPLES: William "Refrigerator" Perry.

Now let's get busy with some easy computations on your daily caloric allowance. The resting metabolic rate for an average male ectomorph and mesomorph is approximately 2,000–2,500 calories. Male endomorphs have a resting metabolic rate of about 1,200–1,500 calories. Consider that roughly 500 calories are burned per hour of weight training and aerobic exercise; it's half that number for endomorphs. You must add calories over and above that resting rate if, in fact, you're looking to build size.

Apply this formula to old "Big Back" Haney. I'm a mesomorph. My resting metabolic rate is 2,500 calories. The typical mesomorph has a resting metabolic rate of 2,000 calories, but I'm not your average mesomorph by any means—I carry a whole lot of muscle mass on my body, way above the norm. Say I train for two hours per day, burning 500 calories per hour. If I want to maintain current size, then, I need to add 1,000 calories—that's 3,500. If I want to pack on any weight, I must add an extra 500–700 calories per day. A 4,000–4,200 calorie allowance is ideal for anyone who trains two hours a day, is ectomorphic or mesomorphic, does not work a physically demanding job, and wants to gain quality muscle-mass. An extreme ectomorph could go even higher—4,200–5,000—and a mesomorph can often get away with 3,400–4,000—my typical off-season allowance. Now I jump to 5,000 calories during the pre-contest phase, but that takes into account the elimination of almost all fats and a corresponding increase in exercise activity as the show draws near.

Always consider the source of those additional calories. Adding a higher percentage of calories from fat will promote an increase in body weight—not in pounds of muscle, but of fat. All calories are not created equal. Follow the ideal percentage breakdown (60 percent carbs, 30 percent protein, 10 percent fat) to stay on-line with sound nutrition as you pack on pounds of lean muscle mass.

Endomorphs must tread lightly in this caloric equation—say your resting metabolic rate is 1,200 and you burn 250, not 500, calories per hour of training. All you should add, then, is an extra 250 calories per day to compensate for each hour of exercise. Endomorphs who follow my advanced program should stay in the 1,800–2,000 range—peaking at 2,500 if your job requires constant physical activity. Most endomorphs should do thirty minutes of aerobic exercise per day at 65–80 percent of their maximum heart rate.

Here's a sample chart to use as a blueprint for your quality-building diet program. Experiment to see what works for you. I've included the women's requirements as a basis for comparison.

MALE

ENDOMORPH (1750 CALORIES PER DAY)

30 percent protein	=	525 calories	=	131 grams
60 percent carbs	=	1050 calories	=	262.2 grams
10 percent fat	=	175 calories	=	19.4 grams

ECTOMORPH/MESOMORPH (3500 CALORIES PER DAY)

30 percent protein	=	1050 calories	=	262 grams
60 percent carbs	=	2100 calories	=	525 grams
10 percent fat	=	350 calories	=	38.8 grams

FEMALE

ENDOMORPH (925 CALORIES PER DAY)

30 percent protein	=	277 calories	=	138.3 grams
60 percent carbs	=	555 calories	=	138.3 grams
10 percent fat	=	102.7 calories	=	11.3 grams

MESOMORPH (1500 CALORIES PER DAY)

30 percent protein	=	450 calories	=	112.2 grams
60 percent carbs	=	900 calories	=	225 grams
10 percent fat	=	150 calories	=	16.4 grams

NOTE: These figures are not etched in stone. Daily caloric allowance will vary from person to person. Use the chart as a guideline; feel free to experiment based on your individual needs.

6

PEAKING

DEPLETION AND RELOADING

One week before the Olympia: A year of strict dieting and heavy training behind me. Am I ready for the ultimate test? I thought back on the past few Olympias, trying to put everything into perspective. The whole process of carbohydrate depletion and reloading rushed in on me like a tidal wave. Man, what a wild trip this can be for a bodybuilder. Let me go over the basic principles behind the depletion and reloading. Then you'll have a better understanding of what I did in '91 that made me so freaky and intense.

Depletion occurs as you drastically lower carbohydrate and water intake, allowing the muscle cells to shrink—this gives your physique a "flat" appearance. During depletion, expect to feel weak and tired; it's as if you've been given a diuretic. You could lose between five to eight pounds. Carefully monitor your caloric intake and weight loss. Increase the protein and fats to replace the carbs missing in your diet—chicken, tuna (no salt), and amino acids on the protein side, almonds and egg yolks on the fat side.

The fun begins six days before a contest. Most bodybuilding shows take place on Saturday night; start depleting on Monday and continue until Wednesday. Never go below 50 grams of carbohydrates and three glasses of water a day.

Exact levels of depletion vary from one person to the next. Let's use Lou Ferrigno as an example. Lou is huge—any man who weighs more than 280 pounds is what I call huge. Fifty grams of carbohydrates and three glasses of water or four cups of hot tea would throw his system into a severe shock, causing disorientation and potential liver and kidney damage. For the huge men of bodybuilding, those of you with longer muscle structures, 150–250 grams of carbs and six or seven cups of hot tea is more like it.

Adjust your training to suit your physical state—if you lower the weight by 20 percent and increase the reps, this depletes the muscle completely.

After three days of depletion, it's time to reverse the process through reloading. Take in at least 50–75 grams of carbs every ninety minutes. I may reload with 100 grams every ninety minutes; you may select a lower figure. Again, it's a personal matter, one that is a function of your individual body type and anatomy.

Reload with rice, oatmeal, potatoes, pasta (complex), and apples and bananas (simple). Avoid dried fruit. Raisins, dates, prunes—even candy bars—will freak out your adrenal glands, throwing your natural balance out of whack. Keep protein constant at 100–150 grams. Green, leafy vegetables help to add fiber and purify the digestive system. Fluid intake remains the same as it did during depletion. Reloading is, again, a three-day process. Slowly but surely the muscle cell will expand. By showtime every muscle should be completely packed with glycogen. Experiment with depletion and reloading five weeks out from a contest. Timing, as usual, is everything.

That's depletion and reloading in a nutshell. If you're wondering why a bodybuilder has to go to such extremes, well, there's only one answer: Look at the photos in this book of the great bodybuilders who tried to wax me at the 1991 show. Unbelievable physiques. Magnificent striations and vascularity. Enough said.

The Final Week

I had to hit depletion and reloading at just the right time—and to the proper degree—if I was going to nail an eighth Olympia title. That's where the questions cropped up: Okay, I remember peaking a week too soon in '86. I know what I did wrong. But, hey, I was only twenty-six years old. My body is different now. I'm thirty-one. Will it react in the same way?

Don't start messing around with all the little details unless you know what you're doing. There's no second chance to get it right. If you screw up, you've screwed up for the entire year. And in my case . . . I'd be screwing up for a lifetime, because I was already at the top of the sport. It's a long way down from the top.

I thought long and hard. I studied the situation. *Okay, let's go for it; I'm going to deplete to no more than 125–150 grams of carbohydrates. I'll start on Monday—not Sunday as in the past—and deplete for three full days. Don't deplete too far. Leave enough margin for error so you'll have enough time to recover.*

So I depleted in the 125–150 grams-of-carb range for three days. I never depleted fully. A hint of the muscle tone remained intact; my legs were still looking nice and crisp—even as late as Wednesday evening.

I started carbohydrate loading Thursday morning around 7 A.M. There was precious little time to put the carbs back in so I had to go for broke—I went up to 800 grams of carbohydrates in the first day of reloading, instead of my usual 450 grams. I had to get the full shock effect of muscle expansion or the Olympia could slip between my fingers; my place in history would be lost.

THURSDAY: The carbs went in—*bam!*
FRIDAY: The carbs went in again—*bam, bam!*
SATURDAY AT 8 A.M: Everything was looking good; the definition was still coming in. And by 1 P.M.—the beginning of the show—it was freaky. Gil Ruiz, who'd watched me from the beginning of my career, was completely blown away. Albert Busek, a leader of the bodybuilding community in Germany and one of the most astute judges of physique champions in the world, told me: "Lee, you are in fantastic shape." That did it. I knew right then and there I was going to break the record.

Reloading is such an amazing experience. Your body basically says: "You've starved me for three days. I'm going to suck up as much glycogen as I can to feed the muscle cell and protect myself from any further funny business (depletion). All of a sudden it's a balloon effect—poof. Your musculature comes into sharp, clear focus. The muscles look so vibrant and alive. The skin is so taut. Totally awesome.

Safety tips for the final week:

- Do not freak out at the last minute and take diuretics or follow unhealthy fads like sodium depletion and sodium reloading.

All of a sudden you're going to throw a bunch of salt into your body? That's ridiculous. If you drop down to zero sodium intake you will cramp on stage.

- Increase mineral supplementation to avoid cramping. Magnesium, potassium, calcium, and zinc are the best options.
- Drink mineral water during depletion and reloading. The water purifies your body, keeps the kidneys functioning properly, and allows protein to travel to the muscle cells for sustained growth.
- Don't put your body through any unnecessary ordeals. Bodybuilding is hard enough as it is. You don't have to suffer permanent injury to win in this sport. Learn from my experience and play it safe.

7
PERFECT POSING

All the training and dieting in the world will fall short of the mark without an impressive, flattering presentation. Posing is a matter of style and substance. Keep in mind that you're both an athlete and an entertainer. Convince the judges and the audience that you're having fun. That's what I do. Put a smile on your face. Project positive energy. That positive energy hits the judges like a lightning bolt.

I've been around the block a few times. Eight Olympia titles taught me a few lessons about what to do—and what not to do—at a show. I see certain bodybuilders leap up on stage with a negative attitude. They scowl. They grimace, as if they intend to attack the judges; frightening the men who evaluate your performance is a questionable strategy.

Exude confidence. Here's what I say to myself when it's showtime: *I've worked hard all year. I've sweated and strived for success. Now I'm ready. This is my night to party. I'm going to strut my stuff—here it is!* This confidence—call it arrogance if you will—spills over to the judges and the crowd.

Believe that you are Number One. Display that self-confidence and poise in your face. Learn to control your facial expressions when you

strike a pose. Relax your facial muscles as you flex; this takes practice.

It all begins with preparation. Do your homework. Study anatomy. Train scientifically and with consistency. If you're unprepared for the contest, then forget the whole deal. Stay home. Go fishing. Cash in your chips. Never do anything to compromise your integrity. Professionalism is the key to success. Again, this relates to your self-confidence. If you arrive with a facial expression that says: *Please, get me out of here; I don't think I'm ready for this,* the judges and the audience will pick up on this self-doubt. You'll be booed off the stage—no questions asked!

The seven mandatory poses: Front double biceps à la Lee Haney.

Lat spread from the front.

Overhead abdomen with big thighs as a bonus.

Lee's patented side chest.

**The triceps pose—
flex to impress.**

Double biceps from behind—freaky!

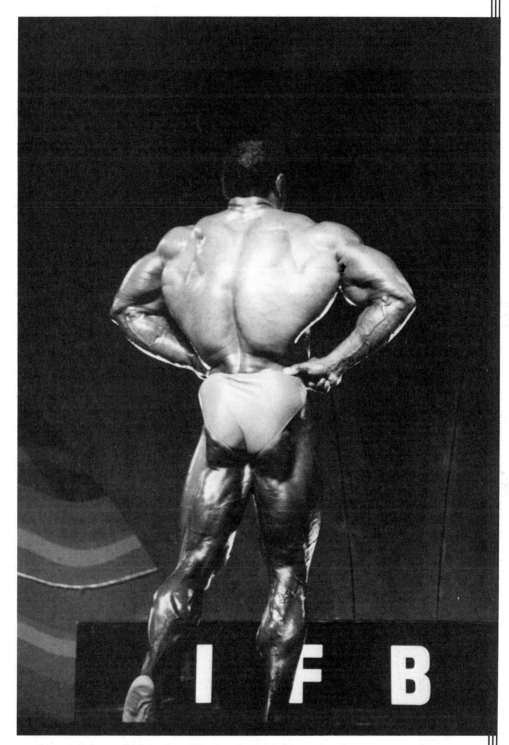

Lat spread from behind—"Big Back" Haney at his best.

THE BASIC ELEMENTS OF POSING

Step One: Learn the seven mandatory poses

1) Double biceps
2) Lat spread from the front
3) Overhead abdomen shot
4) Side chest pose
5) Triceps pose
6) Double biceps from behind
7) Lat spread from behind

I've included photos of each pose for you to analyze and emulate. These seven poses form the basis of your routine. Learn what they are. Rehearse them in front of a mirror—for hours if necessary. Have a friend videotape your posing for further analysis and closer scrutiny.

Step Two: Select a Role Model

Bodybuilding is a sport, much like baseball or basketball. Young baseball players here in Atlanta watch Deion Sanders, Terry Pendleton and Steve Avery and try to pattern themselves after their heroes. Same thing with bodybuilding. I idolized Robby Robinson. I loved the way he hit his double biceps pose, his lat spread, his side chest. I studied his posing style very carefully.

Follow my lead. Pick a role model and try to do everything the way he does it—the mandatory poses, transitions from pose to pose, the little nuances that make his routine unique. Once you've learned from your hero, enlist an experienced competitor—either amateur or professional—to assist you. Soon you'll be able to create your own angle on posing—the flow, the transition from one pose to the next.

Step Three: Be Creative

Creativity is one of the intangibles of a good posing routine. Arnold worked with ballet dancers to fine-tune his transitions, add grace and style to his presentation.

It doesn't matter what route you take to the top. All I ask is that you create something original, a presentation that's organic to who and what you are. I can't say enough about originality. When I hit the stage my presentation must scream: "Here I am! This is Lee Haney at his best." Every angle is perfect. Every transition is clear, logical and dramatic.

Lee Haney displays
the art of creative
posing.

Step Four: Plan Ahead

Never wait until the last minute to fine-tune your posing. I start putting my routine together about six months before a show. Listen to what people are saying about your physique. Make adjustments. Don't be afraid of constructive criticism. Of course, don't fall victim to jealousy or misguided physique bashing, either. In the *Pumping Iron* days it was typical for guys to mislead a rival about his posing style. Be careful.

The judges appreciate a prepared, confident bodybuilder. They want to know that you put considerable time and effort into your posing routine. If they see you waltz onto the stage and just do three or four poses and walk off—no connection between the poses, no flow whatsoever—then it's like, "Next!"

This is your moment. Don't blow it by taking the easy way out. My planning for the 1990 Olympia helped salvage the show, it kept my winning streak intact. My posing routine "Look Out For Number One" was unique. It was powerful. I wasn't in perfect form so my posing took on even more importance. The judges looked at me critically. They compared me to Lee Labrada, my main rival that year. My presentation was so impressive that it convinced them—"Yeah, Lee is still the best bodybuilder in the world. No doubt about it."

Step Five: Select Music Appropriate To Your Physique

Little things do make a difference. Your choice of music is crucial. The music must reflect your personality as a bodybuilder. It's the climax to an entire year of training.

Some guys use soft music to allow them the luxury of showing off their muscularity. Now you don't want to rush a big physique; it requires a certain amount of time to strike each pose and snap out smooth, crisp transitions. But soft music is out of the question. My attitude is to display power, grace, and dominance. Forget the comparisons. Compare what? I am supreme.

That's why I only hit one show a year. My training is focused on that goal to dominate. I give it everything I've got. Passive posing doesn't fit my image. Go with what works for you. If you're not a domineering person on stage, then don't select domineering music. But I honestly believe success in bodybuilding depends on a healthy ego, the conviction that you are the king of the hill. Everybody step back with the sheep. I'm the shepherd of this flock.

Off stage I'm a mild-mannered person. On stage, though, it's "stay out of my way." And my choice of music reflects that perspective. The 1984 Olympia provides an excellent example of this principle in action. As I mentioned earlier, 1983 was extremely frustrating. Placing third in the Olympia was not what I had in mind. Jim Manion, Arnold, and Joe Weider all offered encouragement. Joe told me: "Come back next year and you can take it—if you're ready."

So in selecting the music for 1984 I decided to make a statement: "Arnold is gone. I am the one true dominating force in bodybuilding." I wanted majestic music, something to demonstrate that a reemergence was taking place, that a new king was being coronated. I went with the theme from the movie *Excalibur*. Powerful, dramatic, and evocative. I was under the gun to be in the best shape of my life. I had to be totally awesome.

In the final analysis, the music reinforced all of my training, sweat, and pain. I was, in fact, coronated on that night long ago at Radio City Music Hall. I was the man who would be king—and that was quite a dream to live up to.

Step Six: Pay Attention to All the Little Details

The last few weeks leading up to a show are pretty crazy. You're so focused on training and diet that the last thing you want to worry about is posing. But this is when it matters the most. Work with someone you trust. Have them take pictures of you. Analyze the pictures. Scrutinize videotapes. Don't miss a single detail.

Robert "Superman" Blount is my main man, a training partner who is also an expert poser. He helps me out in the last three weeks before a show. Checking my poses. Watching for the precision of my transitions from one pose into another. Everything! When he tells me I'm ready— that's it, it's time to rock and roll.

Attire is an often overlooked detail. Wear something that fits well and is flattering to your physique. Securely place your privates in your posing trunks to avoid embarrassing situations! Don't allow any bizarre events to detract from your overall presentation.

Tanning is another factor. The better you tan, the better you'll look under the bright lights. Both blacks and whites need to tan evenly and completely. Tanning beds are one option, but natural sunbathing (with adequate safeguards) is the best way to go. Lotions are available—in lieu of tanning—to darken the skin. Technology is improving. Experiment to discover what suits your natural skin coloring.

Applying oil is yet another variable. My personal favorite is Jojoba oil; it has a nice sheen that brings your muscularity into brilliant focus. Put on one coat of oil the night before the event. Remember that all that tanning is drying out your skin; it will soak up the oil like a sponge. Reapply oil again on the morning of the show and before you go on stage.

Step Seven: Be True to Yourself

If you're a big guy like yours truly, then structure your routine to show off the strong, powerful mandatory poses. Concentrate on displaying symmetry and proportion. My double biceps, lat spread, side chest, lat spread from behind, and double biceps are all tremendous. The overhead lat shot (the "Sergio Oliva" pose) and overhead ab shot—well, not my best, but it's not a weak spot, either. I'm fortunate. My natural symmetry has blessed me with flexibility. I can pose from any angle and still impress the judges.

Men who do not have strong, big backs tend to do a lot of poses from the side. They never turn around completely to showcase their Achilles' heel. That's smart. Never highlight your weakest area. I learned this valuable lesson from Mohamed Makkawy. Man, he waxed me all over Europe—including the Mr. Olympia in Munich—in 1983. He was a master poser. You'd never see him doing a lat spread from behind or a double biceps from behind—he'd always strike poses from the side to accentuate his arms and abs, cleverly disguising the fact that he lacked width. What a genius!

The mandatory poses win the shows; that's what you must focus on in your posing routines. Check out the photos in this chapter. Study them carefully. Design a routine that builds on your strengths, not one that exploits your weaknesses.

A GALLERY OF POSES

Albert Beckles—"always ripped, always ready"— demonstrates a front double biceps.

Vince Taylor's front lat spread.

Taylor's side triceps pose—with personality!

Three versions of the double biceps from behind: above, Lee "The Flea" Labrada hits his; above right, Robby Robinson—I idolized him—and loved the way he hit his double biceps from behind; and bottom right, Shawn Ray's version.

Dorian Yates displays a lower back pose.

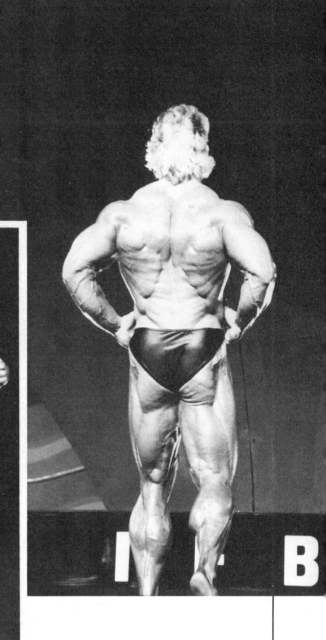

Francis Benfatto exemplifies the ballerina style of posing—a softer display of symmetry.

Rich "The Itch" Gaspari hits an overhead abdomen shot.

Thierry Pastel: Creativity with a French accent.

Sergio Oliva.

Frank Zane.

8

BODYBUILDING FOR ATHLETES

odybuilding and superior athletic performance: The two go hand in hand. Look around professional sports and what do you see?

- Deion Sanders is doing upright rows on Nike commercials.
- Bo Jackson is lifting heavy dumbbells and doing leg work as part of his rehab.
- Baseball and basketball players are hitting the weight room—consistently—year-round.

It's no accident. A selective weight-training program improves muscle strength, muscle endurance and protects joints, tendons and ligaments from injury; aerobic exercise builds stamina for sustained bursts of energy.

Bodybuilding and sports are compatible. There's only one reason why anyone doubts that fact—the mistaken belief that a bodybuilder and a physique champion are identical. Not true. Everyone is capable of being a bodybuilder. You work hard in the gym to improve your physique and enhance strength and vitality.

But how many physique champions do you know? A person who has won show after show under severe scrutiny. A time-tested warrior who trains scientifically for competitive success in the art of presenting the power and beauty of the human body on stage. We're a rare breed.

An athlete should not train like a competitive bodybuilder. But there's much to learn from an expert who understands the workings of the human anatomy, a physique champion with a track record for coming through under pressure.

I've had the pleasure of training three elite athletes: Evander Holyfield, who was preparing to become the Heavyweight Champion; Kevin Willis of the Atlanta Hawks, one of the best rebounders in the NBA; and Gerald Perry, a talented left-handed-hitting first baseman for the St. Louis Cardinals.

These are high-endurance athletes. The nature of their sport dictates a particular training strategy. Serious, yes. But there's no need for any athlete to go through the long, hard workouts of a bodybuilder (the programs listed in chapter 4).

Kevin is jumping up and down every night for forty minutes. I certainly don't want him doing heavy squats the day before or after a game. Evander has his hands up all the time. Why would I have him do 8,000 shoulder presses? He just needs explosive strength for added punching power. I don't want to restrict any of his joints—that's for sure. And Gerald must train like a running back: Run as fast as you can for a set distance and then stop on a dime. His skill requires a blend of explosiveness, cardiovascular fitness, and anaerobic endurance.

Fit the bodybuilding program to the needs of the athlete. It's really quite simple. Three case studies. Three different programs. Take what I did with these athletes and apply the principles to your own sport. Bodybuilding and sports mix perfectly—if you know what you're doing.

EVANDER HOLYFIELD

I worked with Evander for several months in preparation for his bout with Buster Douglas. The outcome was tremendous; Evander nailed Buster with punch after punch en route to the title. Think back to the weigh-in. Evander's physique was sharp and ripped at 217 pounds. Buster's stomach was flopping over his trunks. The poor guy had all the abdominal definition of a Pillsbury Doughboy!

The outcome of the fight was determined at the weigh-in—not just because Evander looked better, but because he was better prepared for battle.

The Weights

A boxer must enhance his explosiveness. That's the secret behind all punching power. With Evander, for example, I'd have him rotate back and forth between an explosive movement and a rhythmic movement. Yes, the advanced bodybuilding principles strike again—with one significant difference: The weight is much lighter. No sense in packing on unnecessary mass that restricts flexibility and range of motion. I'm striving to build functional strength and promote quality muscle growth.

BACK: Only two exercises: wide-grip pulldowns (rhythmic) with high reps (12–15), and barbell bent-over rows (explosive) for 8–10 reps. Explosive movements usually dictate a weight allowing you to lift in the 6–8 rep range. Not for a boxer, though. How much back width does Evander need?

SHOULDERS: Three movements per training session. Either front or behind-the-neck military press (explosive)—he'd alternate between these two from one workout to the next—lateral raises (rhythmic) and upright rows. These four exercises hit the deltoid complex from every angle. Power is generated in the trapezius and transferred through the rear deltoid. Weak shoulders put a fighter at risk of an injury and will minimize the "pop" in his punch.

CHEST: Three movements. Barbell bench press (explosive), incline barbell bench press (explosive), and pec deck (rhythmic). Stimulate, don't annihilate. I did not want to overwhelm him with a tremendous amount of weight. He could bench more than 300, no sweat. But that wasn't the point. Explode with the bar in the bottom position and follow through to the top; visualize exploding forward with a devastating punch. Connect the movement of the weight with the skill in the ring. It's a logical connection.

ARMS: Nothing fancy. Triceps pressdowns (rhythmic) and lying triceps extensions (explosive) with a fairly light weight; barbell curls (explosive) and preacher curls (rhythmic), did the trick for biceps. Again, strength

Heavyweight boxing champion Evander Holyfield. *(Will Hart/ Photofest)*

and endurance supports the integrity of joints, tendons, and ligaments placed under stress in the ring.

LEGS: Leg extensions (rhythmic) for 12–15 reps and squats or 45-degree leg press (explosive) take care of the frontal thigh; leg curls (rhythmic) handle the hamstrings. Evander used a safety squat rack to minimize wear and tear on his knees and back. Legs are an underrated part of a boxer's arsenal. Think it's easy to stay light on your feet—dancing and prancing—while someone is throwing punches at your body and face? Not exactly.

ABDOMINALS: Basic exercises with a twist: I'd have Evander put a weight plate on his midsection to increase the resistance. The guy is getting poked and popped in the stomach with punches; those abs must be strong or he's in deep trouble. Incline sit-ups (weighted), seated crunches and vertical leg raises (with a dumbbell between the feet) for abs; hyperextensions with a weight plate for added lower back strength.

Anaerobic Threshold Training and Plyometrics

A boxer lives and dies on his feet. He must know how to keep moving while he's fighting. It's a subtle art, blending coordination, agility, and speed into a tightly-woven fabric. Once Evander forged a foundation of strength, it was time to convert that raw power into a double whammy of speed and strength.

PLYOMETRICS: When muscles are extended and stretched, then immediately contracted to create a sudden movement—includes any type of jumps, hops, and rebounds that condition the reflexes to fire instantaneously under pressure. Anaerobic threshold training—short bursts of activity so demanding that the muscles must rely on an internal metabolic process for oxygen—simulates a boxer's rapid-fire pacing during a three-minute round.

I decided to combine plyometrics and anaerobic threshold training in the most realistic formula for a boxer—five to ten, three-minute rounds of constant activity. My mission was to get Evander's pulse rate into his max range of 180 or 190 (beats per minute) by the end of the round. Then, after his sixty-second rest interval, the pulse rate would drop to 130. It took time to reach this level of conditioning. Training must be progressive and systematic. Evander couldn't handle the three-minute rounds at first. We slowly advanced from one- to three-minute rounds, carefully preparing his body for the rigors of a championship fight.

Usually Lou Duva and George Benton (Evander's trainers) had him do just a few boxing drills in the morning. Then he'd eat lunch, take a nap, eat a large meal, and then we'd rock and roll. Here's a sample workout:

> Plyometrics: running on his hands, hopping on his hands, alternating with hops, skips and bounding (90 seconds).
> Anaerobic Threshold: Short sprints—backwards, forwards, sideways (90 seconds).

At the end of the training cycle he was doing eight or nine, three-minute rounds. We'd repeat this drill three or four times a week; frequency increased as the fight drew near.

THE STRENGTH CURVE: All athletes have a particular strength curve that represents the physical requirements of their sport. For Evander, that strength curve looks like a checkmark—you go down and then explode up in a sudden movement. I would use the symbol of the checkmark to keep Evander on-line with his plyometric exercises. Say Evander is doing a hopping, skipping, or bounding drill. I would yell at him, "Checkmark, explode! Checkmark, explode!" He then applied the idea of the checkmark (an explosive strength curve) to his punching drills and fighting skills. It reached the point where he'd hear "checkmark, explode" in his mind every time he was ready to go on the attack in the ring. It was one more tactic that helped put him over the top in the Douglas fight.

Overview

I took Evander from 198 to 217 pounds in a period of several months. All quality muscle-mass. No excess fat. Running and other cardiovascular exercise accompanied his morning boxing workouts. An ectomorph, Evander would often take in 5,500–6,000 calories per day. He could get away with that high a level, as his schedule was so frenetic, his training so intense. By fight night—he looked great; lean, hard, and vibrant. And, of course, he beat Buster for the title. The program matched up with his needs, and that was a great feeling for both of us.

EVANDER HOLYFIELD'S PROGRAM+

EXERCISE	SETS	REPS
BACK		
Wide-grip pulldown	3	12–15
Barbell bent-over row	3	8–10
SHOULDERS		
Behind-the-neck military press*	3	8–10
Front military press	3	8–10
Upright row	3	10–12
Lateral raise	3	8–10

CHEST

Barbell bench press	3	8–10
Pec deck	3	12–15
Incline barbell bench press	3	8–10

LEGS

Leg extension	3	12–15
Leg curl	3	12–15
Squat	3	8–10
45-degree leg press	3	8–10

ARMS

Triceps pressdown	3	12–15
Lying triceps extension	3	8–10
Barbell curl	3	8–10
Preacher curl	3	6–8

ABS

Incline sit-up (with weight added)	2–3	15
Seated crunch	2–3	15
Vertical leg raise (with a weight)	2–3	15
Hyperextension (with a weight)	2–3	15

*alternate workouts
#alternate with 45-degree leg press
+ Fred Hatfield, Ph.D., and Chas Jordan assisted me with Evander's training program.

THE SCHEDULE: The on-three, off-one program (Evander always rests on Sunday).

Day #1: Arms, chest, triceps, and abs
Day #2: Legs
Day #3: Back, shoulders, and abs
Day #4: Aerobics

KEVIN WILLIS

Basketball players make a living with their legs. Running and jumping is where it's at, especially for a guy like Kevin who is known as a superb rebounder. Tyrone "Ropeman" Felder and I work with Kevin to increase his vertical jump—through plyometric drills—and enhance his lower body strength via selective resistance training.

Leg extensions (rhythmic), squats (explosive), and 45-degree leg press (explosive) provide the quadriceps strength to support forty minutes of running, leaping, bounding, and jumping. Leg curls (rhythmic), of course, are a staple for hamstrings. All athletes should do leg curls. No excuses!

As with a boxer, it isn't necessary to lift heavy weights on the leg movements. Kevin is not a physique champion searching for mass and cuts; he's an elite athlete in pursuit of maximum minutes and peak performance. "Ropeman" and I always keep the weight light on the squats—why risk an injury to the back and knees?

Kevin's most important requirement—and this is true for most basketball players—is cultivating the explosive, springlike power to propel an athlete off the hardwood for rebounds and follow-up jumpers. That's why he follows the explosive/rhythmic pattern of lifting for each bodypart.

Atlanta Hawks forward Kevin Willis.

Willis Versus Holyfield: A Modified Program

Kevin's upper body routine is similar to Evander's. There is, however, a slight variation in emphasis. Kevin goes high on the reps (15) for lateral raises, while Evander stays in the 10–12 bracket. The high-rep, light-weight strategy prioritizes muscle endurance, not muscle strength. Endurance in the shoulder capsule is a blessing for a hoop star—he always has his hands in the air for rebounding, shooting, and passing.

Kevin is also into lifting heavier weights than Evander. He can play with 315 pounds on the bench press like it's nothing. Chest development is useful in basketball—you're constantly pushing off to improve defensive and/or offensive positioning on the court. And, naturally, the bench press is a pushing movement (see chapter 4).

Biceps and back training also undergo changes from a boxer to a basketball player: Kevin adds concentration curls (he likes to have big arms to intimidate the other guys playing in the paint) and T-bar row and seated cable row for back—quality takes precedence over size.

Overview

Kevin is jumping up and down night after night on the court. A solid weight training, aerobics (see chapter 4) and plyometric program simplifies the biomechanical mission of moving from point A—the hardwood—to point B—the basket. His rebounding totals are steadily increasing as the program pays its dividends. Kevin is another elite athlete who appreciates the benefits of bodybuilding.

KEVIN WILLIS, ATLANTA HAWKS[+]

EXERCISE	SETS	REPS
Barbell bench press	3	8–10
Dumbbell flye	3	8–10
Incline barbell bench press	3	8–10
Front military press	3	8–10
Lateral raise	3	12–15
Triceps pressdown	3	12–15
Lying triceps extension	3	8–10
Barbell curl	3	8–10

Preacher curl	3	8–10
Concentration curl	3	12–15
Wide-grip pulldown	3	12–15
Seated cable row	3	8–10
T-bar row	3	8–10
Leg extension	3	12–15
Leg curl	3	12–15
45-degree leg press	3	8–10
Squat*	3	8–10
Seated crunch	2–3	15–20
Incline sit-up	2–3	15–20

*alternate workouts
⁺Tyrone "Ropeman" Felder assisted me with Kevin's training program.

THE SCHEDULE: A three-day-a-week program based on the foundation-building model (chapter 3):

Monday: Upper body
Wednesday: Lower body
Friday: Upper body
Abs: Every other day.

FOLLOWING WEEK: Arrange schedule so that lower body is worked twice, upper body once.

GERALD PERRY

A talented athlete whose career is in transition. Gerald anchored the Braves infield for several years. Then he moved to Kansas City, where he managed to hit a game-winning grand slam off of Nolan Ryan—another veteran known for his training intensity. Now (at this writing) he's a valuable utility player for the St. Louis Cardinals. Need a left-handed pinch hitter with some pop in his bat? Gerald's the guy. And, thanks to his dedication to training, he can still run the bases pretty well.

I work with Gerald in the off-season. He understands that a lot of younger players want to steal his job. And, unlike some veterans, this thirty-three-year-old Atlanta resident is taking the bull by the horns with an aggressive, productive approach to the aging process.

St. Louis Cardinals first baseman Gerald Perry. *(St. Louis Cardinals)*

The first step is reducing his percentage of body fat with aerobics three times a week and a strict, low-fat diet. Lower body lifting is also crucial to a baseball player's effectiveness. Leg presses and squats provide the explosive speed and quick acceleration needed to run the bases. Rhythmic movements—leg extensions and leg curls for lower body; wide-grip pulldowns, seated cable rows, preacher curls, and dumbbell flyes for upper body—add muscle tone and shape without restricting his range of motion. And, of course, the arm and shoulder lifts enhance his ability to nail runners moving from first to second on the all-important double play.

Functional strength and quality muscle growth without unwanted bulk. Gerald appears bigger than he used to when he played for the Braves. He may weigh more. But he's taut and sharp. No excess baggage around his middle. I set up his program to redistribute his weight, not limit his range of motion or flexibility.

Baseball players can't ignore stretching; it's the simplest path to flexible muscles. Elongate the muscle by focusing on the negative part of the lift. Stretch for ten minutes after each workout. Basic stretches for the quads, hams, shoulders, triceps, and hips keep a baseball player loose and limber; joints, tendons, and ligaments stay prepared for the steady lifting to come.

Knee problems are a ballplayer's worst nightmare. Just look at Ozzie Guillen of the White Sox. The poor guy missed the entire 1992 season. Accidents will happen. But I want to do everything in my power to help Gerald stay out of trouble.

We start each leg workout with light leg extensions, an exercise that strengthens and protects the area surrounding the knees. Then we move to leg presses—not squats—with a light weight. Reps stay high (in the 12–15 range). Nothing too taxing or stressful.

As with Evander and Kevin, I'm still emphasizing explosive power. But baseball players do not need to pump heavy iron. Instead of loading up a bar (for a bent-over row) with 200 pounds, I'll have Gerald explode with a 25-pound dumbbell on the one-arm dumbbell row. He's not after huge, thick lats; the goal is quality muscle growth.

Overview

Gerald's dedication to training and diet will extend his career. Baseball players must lift weights. That's a given. But don't ignore the importance of stretching and sprinting. I disagree with coaches who have ballplayers run distance. Why? Baseball depends on quick bursts of speed. Focus on sprinting and flexibility training instead of cross-country endurance running.

GERALD PERRY, ST. LOUIS CARDINALS[+]

EXERCISE	SETS	REPS
Leg extension	2–4	12–15
Leg curl	2–4	12–15
45-degree leg press	2–4	12–15
Barbell bench press	3	8–10
Incline barbell bench press	3	8–10
Pec deck or Dumbbell flye	3	12–15
Wide-grip pulldown	3	12–15
Seated cable row	3	12–15
One-arm dumbbell row	3	8–10
Triceps pressdown	3	12–15

Lying triceps extension	3	8–10
Barbell curl	3	8–10
Preacher curl	3	8–10
Front military press	3	8–10
Lateral raise	3	10–12
Upright row	3	10–12
Seated crunch	2–3	15–20
Incline sit-up	2–3	15–20

+ Chas Jordan assisted me with Gerald's training program.

THE SCHEDULE: Gerald adheres to the same three-day-a-week lifting schedule as Kevin. He'll do aerobic work on an off day. Or, if pressed for time, in conjunction with an upper-body workout.

9
THE WILL AND THE WAY

A champion. An eight-time Mr. Olympia. Breaking Arnold's record proves that I'm the best bodybuilder in the history of the sport.

When I hit the stage at the '91 Olympia I feared nothing. My spiritual side clicked in. I had faith. Just do your best and everything will take care of itself. Win, lose, or draw—heck, you're still a winner in my book if you've done everything within your power to succeed.

It's natural to play back the last few weeks leading up to a contest. Josh's birthday took place one week before the '91 Olympia. He was munching on a big chocolate chip cookie. Should I share this cookie with my son on a special occasion? I went with what my heart told me to do: *Lord, bless this chocolate chip cookie; I'm going to eat a piece in celebration of my son's birthday.* The cookie didn't hurt me. In fact, maybe it even helped me a little; it made me feel good inside.

There's more to being a champion than just building impressive muscles. I've had the opportunity to meet a lot of people, travel to many wonderful places. My legacy to the sport of bodybuilding is setting a positive example for young athletes. I preach that bodybuilders can lead holistic, balanced lives, enjoy the blessings of a wife and family; and don't be afraid to admit that you have a spiritual side.

Life is a test—the ultimate test. My belief in God—my faith in salvation—and my commitment to honest hard work guides me through each day. All material things—the gold, the house, the stardom—fade away. The spiritual energy—the people you touch along the way—is all you take with you when you die. Caring for people. That's what makes a true champion.

I like to think that I've set a good example. That was my promise to God when I was only 16: *If you bring me to the pinnacle of success, I will do my best to fulfill the promise of honesty, integrity and caring.*

When you talk about this spiritual stuff a lot of people think you're crazy. But that is where it's at for Lee Haney. Many athletes lose their way after they attain success. Don't let that happen to you.

THE LEE HANEY HOTLINE

Lee Haney offers insights on bodybuilding, nutrition and motivation through a new 900 phone service. Dial 1-900-454-4533 to select the Haney instructional program that interests you the most; the cost is $2 per minute; callers must be 18 years of age or older.

INDEX